So many people I love are still blinded. It is my desire that they too will come to know what the Bible says and Who God really is and that they will trust in Him and give Him their hearts. I believe if you read what I have written that you too will better understand what the truth is. Jesus in His great intercessory prayer in John 17 said "Sanctify them through thy truth: thy word is truth." He does not want us to be deceived. He wants us to know Him and the amazing blessing of His salvation.

It matters how we see God and how we see ourselves. If the way we see God and the way we see ourselves is distorted, we are bound. Lies bind, and God's truth sets us free.

If you do not understand the doctrines of the Bible you are at risk. You are at risk of believing so many lies that are permeating our culture today. Whether we chose to accept it or not, absolute truth exists – and it is found only in God's Word. The world is preparing to accept "the lawless one", the Antichrist. It warns us in 2 Thessalonians 2: 9-11, "Even him, whose coming is after the working of Satan with all power and signs and lying wonders, and with all deceivableness of unrighteousness in them that perish; because they received not the love of the truth, that they might be saved. And for this cause God shall send them strong delusion, that they should believe a lie."

We have enjoyed greater freedom and prosperity in this nation than any other in the history of the world. We have the Word of God. We have the freedom to worship God in spirit and in truth. Do we realize how wealthy we are? Do we realize that it could all go away?

I lived in a delusion of false belief for years. Only the Word of God could set me free. I have written this book to answer the questions I was left with after realizing that Mormon doctrine was false. Now I know how wealthy I am because I have God's Word and know how valuable it is. All throughout the New Testament there are warnings about false teachers and false prophets. There is another gospel spoken of in Galatians. I believed another gospel. If I had understood what was true, then I would not have been deceived by the lie. Only in understanding and knowing true doctrine are we protected from believing false doctrine. I would ask you are you protected by your understanding of the truth?

Jesus, but the Jesus I was taught about was not the Almighty God of the Universe. He was my elder spirit brother. He was not the Jesus of the Bible.

As a Mormon, I was told I was a Christian. The name of Jesus Christ was in the name of the church – The Church of Jesus Christ of Latter-day Saints. I knew many Christians over these years. I believe they accepted me as believing in the same Jesus that they believed in. In reality though, they had no idea what I really believed.

I had been blinded by the "light". It is written in 2 Corinthians that Satan himself is transformed into an angel of light (2 Cor. 11: 14). As a Mormon I was in the "lightest darkest" place I could have been. So much about Mormonism seems right and appears to be similar to Christianity. When Mormon doctrine however is held up against the Bible – it is seen for what it is. It is a well crafted Gnostic imitation of true Christianity. Nothing about it is Christian. In many ways it is more similar to Islam than it is to Christianity.

Only the true Word of God – the Bible had the power to remove my blindness. It says in John 8: 32, "ye shall know the truth, and the truth shall make you free."

God wants us to worship Him "in spirit and in truth" (John 4: 24). He has given us His Word – the Bible so we can know Him. At the request of my husband in 2008 I put down the Book of Mormon, the Doctrine and Covenants, and the Pearl of Great Price (Mormon Scripture) and began an intensive study of the New Testament. After about a year I asked God to know the truth about Mormon doctrine. Miraculously on Easter Sunday in 2009 God removed my blindness. His Word opened my eyes and set me free.

2

INTRODUCTION

For over thirty years I carried a Bible to Church with me. I read some of it, but never knew how precious and valuable it was. I had been told it had been translated incorrectly. I had been told that the Book of Mormon was the most correct book on the earth. After being introduced to Mormonism in 1972, I was told that Joseph Smith was a true prophet of God. I was taught that all Mormon men hold the Melchizedek Priesthood and have the power and authority of God. I was taught that Mormon temples were houses of God and were the most sacred places on earth. I was told that God was once a man and had elevated himself to become God. I was taught that we all were to become gods, and that there were many gods. I was taught that God wanted me to enter into covenants with Him that He would only fulfill if I was faithful, and would severely judge me if I did not obey those covenants. I was taught that God wanted us to obey His laws and ordinances. I had no idea what grace was. I was taught that the church was a perfect organization; restored to earth with the power to grant salvation/exaltation and to take it away. I was taught that there was no salvation outside of the church.

I was never told as a Mormon how to find salvation in Jesus Christ, in believing that He paid for my sins on the cross and that I needed to repent and trust in Him and ask Him to be my Savior. I was taught about

TABLE OF CONTENTS

Mormon Doctrine vs. The Bible: TEKEL – Weighed in the Balance and Found Wanting
Shawna K. Lindsey

DEDICATION

TO MY LORD JESUS CHRIST WHO

ALONE GIVES US HIS AMAZING GRACE

ACKNOWLEDGMENTS

To my husband Larry Lindsey for challenging me to read and study the New Testament. To all the staff at Dallas Bay Baptist Church, especially Pastor Ken Duggan, Pastor David McNabb, and Bob Williams. To Lance, Rochelle, Jennifer, Damon, Micah, Justice, and Silas, for their support and love. For Tom and Linda Lundy for their support and encouragement. To John and Sheila Morgan for wonderful Bible lessons. To members of the Gatekeepers Sunday School class, especially Lon and Nancy Ellis for all their prayers and support. For Pastor Charlie Robertson and his wife Mary for their love and encouragement. To the staff and faculty of Covington Theological Seminary, especially Dr. James Hutchings and Karen Jenkins for their encouragement. To all the Mormons I know and love.

CHAPTER 1: THE INERRANT BIBLE

The Bible is unique. It is different than any other book. The God of the universe, the One and Only true and living God has revealed Himself to us through His Word – the Bible. It is God's inspired Word for His creation – mankind. As a document of history it has been shown to be authentic and genuine. The transmission of the Old Testament is unlike that of any other historical document. There is a unity of the Bible that is unparalleled in any other book. Archaeological findings support the accuracy of people, places, and events in the Bible, especially those manuscripts found in Qumran – the Dead Sea Scrolls. A study of biblical canonization supports the claim of the divine authority of the Bible. The issue of biblical inerrancy is one that lends tremendous strength to the conclusion that the Bible contains all we need to know about the God of the universe and how He has manifested Himself to us in His Son Jesus Christ for our salvation.

That the Bible is unique and distinct from any other book in the world is a fact that few people know much about. The Bible was not written over the period of one man's life as are most books, but over a period of 1,500 years.[1] It did not have only one author or several authors like other books, but was written by over forty authors who had varied backgrounds and life stories.[2] The Bible was not written in one location but on three different continents, including Europe, Africa and Asia.[3] It was written in three different languages: Greek, Aramaic and Hebrew.[4] It was written in times of war, as well as in times of peace, and it was written in different literary genres such as narrative, history, poetry and prophecy.[5] Although the Bible is diverse in these many ways, it presents an unbroken story of the one true and living God, making Himself known through His Son Jesus Christ.[6] There is no other book in existence today that can claim so many unique features.

The Bible is inspired by God. It states in 2 Timothy 3: 16, "All Scripture is inspired by God and is profitable for teaching, for reproof, for correction, and for training in righteousness." And 1 Corinthians 2: 13 says, "No prophecy ever came by the impulse of man, but men moved by the Holy Spirit spoke from God."[7] God's Holy Spirit inspired various men, over time, to write His Word. The words that the authors of the Bible wrote were inspired by the Spirit of God. God spoke His authoritative word through these men, but it was not in them as men that His authority was found, but in His word alone.[8] The men who wrote the Bible did not do so from their own motivation and inspiration. God inspired them to write down what they wrote, in their particular style and vocabulary, not as a secretary would do when taking dictation from someone, but as an author fully engaged in the literary exercise.[9] God worked through His Holy Spirit to inspire their hearts and minds, to write the truth, as He revealed it to them. In John 17: 17 Jesus said "Thy Word is truth." As God revealed truth to men, they wrote, as their minds were inspired and engaged with truth.[10] In 2 Samuel 23: 2, David declared, "The Spirit of the Lord spoke by me, and His word was in my tongue." David recognized that it was God who was inspiring him, and not just himself. It states in 2 Peter 1: 21, "Holy men of God were moved along by the Holy Spirit." These men were moved upon by God's Spirit, to write the truth that God gave them. They did not become someone else when writing God's Word, but wrote from their own emotions and personalities.[11] 2 Timothy 3: 16 could be read as, "All Scripture is God-breathed," because the Greek word 'theopneustos' is derived from the words 'God' and 'breath' – meaning what comes out of the mouth of God.[12] A critical fact is that the writings and not the writers themselves were what was inspired.[13] These men had no inspiration that came from themselves, but only as what came from the Holy Spirit of God acting upon them.

The Bible is genuine, as well as authentic. The genuineness of the Bible relates to the truth of its origin or authorship. This answers the question: Was it truly written by who it was truly written by?[14] The authenticity of the Bible considers, whether the content and facts of the Bible are true.[15] The Bible should be considered, in light of its accuracy in historical facts, as any other book of historical importance should be.[16] In order to determine authenticity, historians use the following criteria: "1. Are any original documents in our hands, or only copies? 2. If only copies exist, how old are they when compared with the approximate date of the original document? (The closer the copies are to the original, the better the chances of higher accuracy) 3. How many copies exist?"[17] When considering how many copies exist, when compared to the manuscripts of the New Testament, it can be considered that Homer's Iliad is one of the "best attested manuscripts of ancient history." There are 643 copies of early manuscripts of Homer's Iliad known to be in existence, and the oldest copies were "copied 500 years after Homer wrote the original manuscript. However, over 24,970 copies of portions of the New Testament exist, and in some cases less than 50 years separate the original New Testament manuscript, and the earliest transcribed manuscript known to us today."[18] Sir Fredrick Kenyon, principal librarian and director of the British museum, stated "In no other case is the interval of time between the composition of the book and the date of the earliest extant manuscript so short as in that of the New Testament. The books of the New Testament were written in the latter part of the first century; the earliest extant manuscripts are of the fourth century – say from 250 to 300 years later...The interval then between the dates of the original composition and earliest extant evidence becomes so small as to be in fact negligible, and the last foundation for any doubt that the Scriptures have come down to us substantially as they were written has now been removed. Both the authenticity and the general integrity of the books of the New Testament may be regarded as finally established."[19] William F. Albright, one of the world's most renowned biblical archaeologists stated, "No other work from Greco-Roman antiquity is so well attested by manuscript tradition as the New Testament. There are many more early manuscripts of the New Testament than there are of any classical author, and the oldest extensive remains of it date only about two centuries after their original composition."[20] F.E. Peters stated, "On the basis of manuscript tradition alone, the works that made up the Christians' New Testament were the most frequently copied and widely circulated books of antiquity." Only counting Greek copies, there are 5,656 partial and complete manuscript portions of the New Testament, which were copied by hand from the second through the fifteenth centuries.[21] There are three basic principles used to test the historic reliability of a document. These are the Bibliographical test, the internal evidence test, and the external evidence test.[22] The bibliographical test examines the transmission of the text by which the documents pass, over time, as well as how reliable are the available copies, in regard to the number of manuscripts, and what is the time interval between the original and the existing copies?[23] Regarding the internal evidence test for the reliability of the New Testament, Aristotle's dictum that "the benefit of the doubt is to be given to the document itself" is still followed today. It is asked if the document is free of known contradictions.[24] The external evidence test for the reliability of the New Testament, asks whether other historical writings affirm or refute what is written in the New Testament. Other sources that may corroborate its "accuracy, reliability, and authenticity" are considered. External evidence, such as early Christian writings by Eusebius, Papias, Irenaeus, Clement of Rome, and Ignatius, serve to validate the New Testament. Michael Wilkins and J.P. Moreland have concluded, that even without early Christian writings, when considering such non-Christian writings of Josephus, Tacitus, Pliny the Younger, as well as the Talmud, if could be determined that "1. Jesus was a Jewish teacher; 2. Many people believed that he performed healings and exorcisms; 3. He was rejected by the Jewish leaders; 4. He was crucified under Pontius Pilate in the reign of Tiberius; 5. Despite this shameful death, his followers, who believed that he was still alive, spread beyond Palestine so that there were multitudes of them in Rome by A.D. 64; 6. All kinds of people from the cities and countryside – men and women, slave and free – worshipped him as God by the beginning of the second century."[25] Josephus wrote about the resurrection of Christ – "At this time there was a wise man called Jesus, and his conduct was good and he was known to be virtuous...Pilate condemned him to be crucified and die. But those who had become his disciples did not abandon his discipleship. They reported that he had appeared to them three days after his crucifixion, and that he was alive."[26]

Biblical archaeology has supported the genuineness and authenticity of the Bible. William Foxwell Albright, a world renowned biblical archaeologist stated "in my opinion, every book of the New Testament was written by a baptized Jew between the forties and the eighties of the first century A.D.". He concluded, that because of the Dead Sea Scroll discoveries at Qumran, the "New Testament proves to be in fact what it was formerly believed to be: the teaching of Christ and His immediate followers between cir. 25 and cir. 80 A.D.".[27] Nelson Glueck, a renowned Jewish archaeologist pronounced, "It may be stated categorically that no archaeological discovery has ever controverted a biblical reference."[28] William F. Albright wrote, "Archaeological discoveries of the past generation in Egypt, Syria, and Palestine have gone far to establish the uniqueness of early Christianity as an historical phenomenon."[29] Millar Burrows of Yale University stated, "The excessive skepticism of many liberal theologians stems not from a careful evaluation of the available data, but from an enormous predisposition against the supernatural...and he adds...on the whole, however, archaeological work has unquestionably strengthened confidence in the reliability of the Scriptural record. More than one archaeologist has found his respect for the Bible increased by the experience of excavation in Palestine. On the whole such evidence as archaeology has afforded thus far, especially by providing additional and older manuscripts of the books of the Bible, strengthens our confidence in the accuracy with which the text has been transmitted through the centuries."[30] It has been stated by Dr. Henry Morris, a Christian apologist and scientist, that "It must be extremely significant that, in view of the great mass of corroborative evidence regarding the biblical history of these periods, there exists today not one unquestionable find of archaeology that proves the Bible to be in error at any point."[31] An amazing fact is also, that the people, places, and events spoken of in the

Bible, are found where the Scripture locates them.[32] The chronology and geography in the Bible, as well as the description of the rise and fall of empires, match up with the information from secular history.[33]

Regarding the Qumran discovery, between the years 150 B.C. to A.D. 70, a monastic group of Jews lived northwest of the Dead Sea, in the Judean hills near Qumran. One of the books they studied and lived by, was the Old Testament. In A.D. 70, when they realized that the Roman armies were coming upon Palestine, they hid their scrolls in the surrounding caves. In 1947, a young shepherd boy found these scrolls within jars, inside the caves. In all, five hundred books were eventually found. About one hundred of these scrolls record parts of the Old Testament, written in Hebrew. These contained all of Isaiah, and parts of every other Old Testament book, except Esther. These scrolls were tested scientifically, and found to be dated from about 150 B.C. When the Dead Sea scroll text of Isaiah was compared to the "Masoretic" manuscripts of one thousand years later, they both read almost exactly the same. The same was true of all the rest of the fragments of each Old Testament book, when compared to the Masoretic text.[34]

The accuracy, of the transmission of the Hebrew Old Testament, over many centuries, is unrivaled. All the way back to the time of Ezra, around 450 B.C., there were special groups or "guilds of scribes", whose job it was to preserve and pass along an "error free" Scriptural text, from one generation to another. These scribes had such a respect for the written Word of God, that even a single minor error in copying, was considered a sin. If only one error was made, the entire manuscript was destroyed. In centuries following, there were Jewish scholars, called Masoretes, whose job it was to carefully examine all known copies of the Old Testament, looking for any and every error. They would remove any copies that were not perfect, so that there would be no transmission of any errors. By their meticulous care, they were able to preserve the continuation of a "virtually pure" Old Testament text. In their insuring exactness in transmission, the Masoretes had developed a system of "markings and notes", that they wrote in the margin of the manuscripts, which would be used by the next person copying the text. They would note things such as "the number of times each letter of the alphabet occurred in each book, the middle letter of the alphabet which occurred in each book, the middle letter of the scroll's Pentateuch, and the middle letter of each page, and a count of letters and words in each column."[35] The leaders, among the Jews living in Palestine and Babylonia during the centuries before Christ, who were responsible for making copies of the Old Testament, were the first to divide the thirty-nine scrolls of the Old Testament into smaller groups, considered "The Law, The Prophets, and The Writings".[36] Jesus, Himself, taught that God was the author of the Hebrew Old Testament. He quoted, as "authoritative or authentic", most of the twenty-two books of the Hebrew Old Testament. He recognized every section including the "Law and Prophets", as well as the "Law, Prophets, and Psalms" (Luke 24: 27, 44) to be prophetically speaking of Him. He "believed" that God's inspiration extended from Genesis through Chronicles (Matthew 23: 35). He set forth the concept, that the Old Testament as a whole, was "unbreakable Scripture" (John 10: 35), and that it would never perish (Matthew 5: 18). He asserted that it must be fulfilled (Luke 24: 44). He, Himself "authenticated" people and events from Eden (Matthew 19: 5), to Jonah and the whale (Matthew 12: 40), including Daniel the prophet (Matthew 24: 15), Noah and the flood (Luke 17: 27), and Sodom's destruction (Luke 17: 29).[37]

There are 1,500 direct or indirect statements in the Bible, that claim that the Bible is of divine origin.[38] God's message to us in the Bible, does not contradict itself. When looking at the sixty-six books of the Bible, for consistency in message, there is an undeniable unity that emerges. There is a unity of authorship, theme, structure, and symbolism. Considering the unity of authorship, the Bible, "evolved over 15 centuries, was written in 3 different languages, was written by 40 different divinely inspired men from a variety of occupations, and was penned under different circumstances and in different countries and cultures, and it discussed diverse theological matters."[39] There is a unity of theme in the Bible, that concerns Jesus Christ, and the redemption He brought. From the earliest hint of the Gospel in Genesis 3: 15, to Revelation 22: 20 "Even so, come, Lord Jesus!" the Bible has an "integrated storyline". "Like a garment woven with many different threads, but all contributing to the shape of the whole, so the Bible has sixty-six books all contributing to one grand design."[40] There is a unity of structure in the Bible. A statement that is spoken of the Bible is, "The New is In the Old concealed; the Old is in the New revealed."[41] In the New Testament, there are 180 quotations from the Old Testament, in addition to references to Old Testament people and events. The Old Testament "points" the reader forward, to a future time when God would personally redeem humanity. The two testaments cannot be separated, without destroying the entire message of the Bible.[42] There is unity of symbolism in the Bible. For example, leaven is used in both the Old and New Testaments, as a symbol for evil.[43] It is as if, various pieces of a cathedral arriving from different cities and countries, come together in a central location, and these pieces are from forty different sculptors over a period of hundreds of years, but all the pieces fit together to form a "single magnificent structure."[44]

Considering the canon of the Bible, the word "canon" comes from the root word "reed" (English word cane, Hebrew form ganeh, and

Greek form kanon). The reed was used as a rod, to measure something, and this word over time came to mean "standard".[45] Jesus, Himself, defined the limits of the canon (the twenty-two books of the Hebrew Old Testament). He also established the principle of canonicity, in that the canon is made up of the "Word of God". Jesus referenced the Old Testament as the "Word of God" in Mark 7: 13, and that which "God said" in Matthew 19: 5, and that which is spoken "by the Spirit" in Matthew 22: 43 and Mark 12: 36. Regarding the New Testament, Jesus assured that the Holy Spirit would direct the apostles into "all the truth" in John 16: 13 and also bring all things that He had taught them to their remembrance in John 14: 26.[46] Canonicity is not determined by man, but by God. The reason that there are only sixty-six books in the Bible is because God inspired that number of books. Only these sixty-six books were given God's divine stamp of authority. So a specific book was not considered canonical because it was determined by men to be valuable. It is canonical not because it is inspiring, but because it is inspired.[47] It is not the "antiquity, authenticity or even religious value" that determines a book's canonicity, but it is inherently valuable because it is canonical. Its canonicity is established or determined solely on God's authority, and not on man's authority.[48] In order to have the correct perspective or canonicity, one must understand that the authority of the Scriptures is not derived from the authority of the church, but the authority of the church is completely based on the authority of the Scriptures. It is not correct to place the church over the canon. God is the One Who has regulated the canon, and man has only recognized the divine authority that God gave to the canon – "God determined the canon, and man discovered it."[49] It is critical to understand that the church did not create the canon; it only recognized which books were inspired by God, and thus had God's divine authority. It can be said, that "a book is not the Word of God because it is accepted by the people of God; rather, it

was accepted by the people of God, because it was the Word of God."
God gives a book its divine authority, and people only recognize its
divine authority.[50] When the question is posed – How did man discover
what God had done regarding inspiration of Scripture? And specifically,
how did the Church Fathers know when they had come upon a
canonical book? There are five principles to consider in the historical
and biblical process of canonization. These are: 1. Is it authoritative –
did it come with the authority of God? 2. Is it prophetic – was it written
by a man of God? 3. Is it authentic – did it tell the truth about God, man,
etc.? 4. Is it dynamic – did it come with the life-transforming power of
God? 5. Was it received, collected, read and used – was it accepted by
the people of God? If these five principles were not present, the book
was not accepted as canonical. In using these principles, the Church
Fathers were directed by the Spirit of God to search all the recorded
religious literature, so they could discover which specific books God had
determined to be canonical.[51]

Considering the development of the Hebrew canon of the Old
Testament, historically there were three principles being used: "1.
Inspiration by God. 2. Recognition by men of God; and 3. Collection and
preservation of the books by the people of God." Regarding inspiration
by God, there are only thirty-nine books in the Old Testament canon,
because these are all that God inspired. In the recognition by men of
God, after God gave a book its authority, men of God gave assent to
that authority by their recognition of it as a prophetic utterance."[52]
When referring to the collection and preservation of the people of God
– "Moses' books were collected and preserved beside the ark (Deut. 31:
26). It states in 1 Samuel 10: 25, that "Samuel told the people the rights
and duties of the kingship; and he wrote them in a book, (literally, the
book) and laid it up before the Lord." Daniel in his day, had a collection

of "the books", and there is evidence that there was a rule used to collect prophetic writings. In the days of Josiah, the "law of Moses" was "found in the house of the Lord" as is written in 2 Kings 23: 24. Proverbs 25: 1 references the proverbs of Solomon being copied by the men of Hezekiah. Ezra kept a copy of the Law of Moses that he had brought out of Babylonian captivity with him, as written about in Ezra chapter 7.[53] The prophetic writings of the Old Testament ended with Malachi. This is supported by the following points: Some of the post exilic prophets claimed, that the next revelation from God, would be immediately before the coming of the Messiah (Mal. 4: 5). They also alluded to the fact that there would be no true prophets during the "intervening" period (Zech. 13: 2-5). Writings from the Maccabean period (between the testaments), show that the people were waiting "until a prophet should arise." Even a book called the Manual of Discipline from the Jews at Qumran reveals that they were also looking for the "coming of a prophet." Josephus' writings even state, that "after the latter prophets Haggai, Zechariah, and Malachi, the Holy Spirit departed from Israel." The New Testament does not quote a book after Malachi as being canonical, and uses the expression "from...Abel to...Zechariah in Matthew 23: 35, which includes only the books from Genesis to II Chronicles.[54] The canon of the Old Testament was most likely finished by about 400 B.C. By 200 B.C., the twenty-two books that had been through the three above principles of canonization were viewed as divided into the Law, the Prophets, and the Writings.[55] The Old Testament is, for the most part, a biographical account of a people, and God's dealings with those people. It was written primarily in Hebrew, which was especially suitable for a biographical focus, because Hebrew is a "pictorial" language, which speaks with vivid and bold metaphors, that both challenges and dramatizes a story. Hebrew has a unique ability of being able to present "pictures" of the events which are written about. It could be said, that a Hebrew "thought in pictures", using nouns that were both concrete and vivid.[56] Hebrew can also be considered a personal language. It speaks to the emotions and the heart, more than to reason and the mind. Its message is said to be "felt", rather than "thought".[57] The theologian F.F. Bruce wrote, "Biblical Hebrew does not deal with abstractions, but with the facts of experience. It is the right sort of language for the record of the self-revelation of a God, Who does not make Himself known by philosophical propositions, but by controlling and intervening in the course of human history. Hebrew is not afraid to use daring anthropomorphisms when speaking of God. If God imparts to men the knowledge of Himself, He chooses to do so most effectively in terms of human life and human language."[58]

In the process of the canonization by the Church Fathers, five principles were previously mentioned. The first principle was the asking of whether the book was authoritative or not. They would have asked: Does this book come with a divine "Thus saith the Lord?" They would also have asked: Does it have a self-vindicating authority that commands attention as it communicates? The second principle was asking if the book was prophetic and was it written by a man of God. The Church Fathers considered whether the book was written by either a prophet or an apostle. The third principle considered whether the book was authentic or not. They may have asked, "Does the book tell the truth about God, man, etc., as it is already known by previous revelation?" and "is it a record of facts as they actually occurred?" The book could not contradict truth. The forth principle concerned whether the book was dynamic or not. It would also be determined if it came with the power of God? The Church Fathers believed that the Word of God was "living and active" (Hebrews 4: 12), and should have a "transforming force for edification" (2 Tim. 3: 16), as well as evangelization (1 Peter 1: 23). The fifth and last principle was whether it was received and generally accepted by the people of God. This acceptance included initial acceptance, as well as final acceptance by the universal church. Every one of the above five principles were needed to prove the canonicity of each book.[59]

The New Testament was written in Greek. The Greek language was suitable for evangelical purposes. It was appropriate for "propositionalizing and propagating" the truth about Jesus Christ, for a couple of reasons. One reason was that Greek was an intellectual language. It was more a language of the mind, than a language of the heart. It was more able to present the codification of communication or reflection on a revelation of God than Hebrew was. It was used to express the "propositional truth" of the New Testament. It had a "technical precision", that was not found in Hebrew. Secondly, Greek was an almost universal language. It was a language that was spoken widely throughout the world.[60]

The recognition of the canonicity of the New Testament was not a "mere mechanical matter settled by a synod or ecclesiastical council." It was a process, directed by the Spirit of God, as God "witnessed to the church about the reality of the Word of God." The Holy Spirit of God opened the eyes of man's understanding, to be able to recognize His Word. The witness of God's Spirit, only "established the reality of the canon, not its extents or limits." The process of canonization was made up of both science and faith.[61] The "determining factor" in the canonization of the New Testament, was inspiration with the primary test being apostolicity. If a book had apostolic authority, then its authenticity and veracity would not be questioned.[62] F.F. Bruce stated "when at last a Church Council – the Synod of Hippo in A.D. 393 –, listed the twenty-seven books of the New Testament, it did not confer upon them any authority which they did already possess, but simply recorded their previously established canonicity (The ruling of the Synod of Hippo was re-promulgated four years later by the Third Synod of Carthage). Since that time, there has been no serious questioning of the twenty-seven accepted books of the New Testament, by Roman Catholics, Protestants, or the Eastern Orthodox Church."[63]

The word "Bible" comes from the Greek word "biblion" which means book. After the Old and New Testaments were brought together, Greek speaking Christians called it the "biblia", the "books". The Christians, who spoke Latin, referred to it as "biblia", as a singular word. Christians from the earliest centuries recognized the unity of the Scriptures, calling it Bible.[64] While the New Testament books were being written, the Old Testament was referred to as the "Scriptures" (Matt. 21:42). This was the term that Jesus and His apostles used for the Old Testament. About twenty years after Christ's ascension to heaven, God's Spirit began to inspire men to write more Scripture. These "autographs" were historical accounts and letters, which would eventually be brought together as the New Testament.[65] By the end of the first century A.D., all of the twenty-seven scrolls of the future New Testament had been finished, but they were in various places throughout the Christian world. The anti-Christian emperor Diocletian, in A.D. 303, decreed that all church buildings should be razed to the ground, and all Scriptures should be destroyed by fire. This event helped to motivate Christians to decide which books would be brought together as the New Testament. Twenty-five years later, Constantine, the Christian emperor, actually "encouraged and sponsored the copying and preserving of Bibles." In A.D. 367, the Bishop Athanasius made the first known list of the twenty-seven books of the New Testament. Jerome, Augustine, the Council of Hippo, and the Third Council of Carthage in turn, all recognized the twenty-seven books as the New Testament canon.[66]

The authors of the Bible used the same materials to write with, as other writers of their time. These writing materials included papyrus, which was a "paper-like material" that was made of the inner bark of a reed plant. Most likely, all the Bible autographs were written on rolls of papyrus. These autographs, under God's protection, were copied before they "perished", and through many centuries, the copies have been re-copied many times. Parchment was also used. It was more durable than papyrus, and was made out of the dried skin of animals. The "most substantial" ancient copies of biblical text are on parchment. The authors wrote, using pen and ink, as is referenced in 3 John 13. The parchments, or papyruses, that were written on, were glued or sewn together making rolls, which were thirty to ninety feet long.[67] The scrolls were subject to being destroyed by fire, water, termites, rot, mishandling, or other deliberate efforts by enemies of God. God, however, preserved His Word, and the process of its transmission. Until the year 1456, after the printing press was invented by Johannes Gutenberg, single copies of the Bible were copied by hand.[68]

For various reasons, only a few Hebrew copies of Scripture survived several centuries after the time of Christ. The Old Testament portion of the English bible of today is based on Hebrew manuscripts, which were written after A.D. 890. These manuscripts are called codex, which means that they are in page form rather than scroll form. These codex include: 1. Cairo Codex (A.D. 895), which is the oldest known Masoretic manuscript of the prophetic books. 2. Leningrad Codex of the Prophets (A.D. 916). 3. Akeppo Codex (A.D. 930), which is a codex of the whole Bible, and is considered the most valuable Hebrew manuscript. 4.

Leningrad Codex (A.D. 1008), which is the largest complete Hebrew manuscript of the Old Testament. The Old Testament was translated into Greek in Alexandria, Egypt, around 180 B.C. The Jews living there spoke Greek, and they wanted to be able to read their Hebrew Scriptures in their native language of Greek. This Greek version of the Old Testament is called the Septuagint. Two Greek manuscripts of the entire Bible were found during the mid 1800's. These were called Codex Sinaiticus and Codex Vaticanus. The Old Testament in these manuscripts is written in Greek or Septuagint form. These manuscripts had been copied by scribes around 400 A.D.[69]

The integrity of the Old Testament is made obvious in part, by the meticulous procedures of transmission that were utilized for centuries. The authenticity and integrity of the New Testament is established in the abundance of high quality copies that have been passed down through the ages. Some of the greatest New Testament discoveries in archaeology have been the uncovering of more than five thousand Greek manuscripts. These are of two different kinds: papyrus fragments (A.D. 100-300), and primary uncials (A.D. 300ff.).[70]

The conviction that the Bible was the inerrant Word of God, with God's divine authority, was one that was held by Christians and Christian teachers throughout the first 1,700 years of church history. The church, and the synagogue, in the time following the apostolic age, held the same view of Scripture. "Normative Tannaite Judaism" claimed to have taught nothing other than that which they found either explicitly or implicitly in the Old Testament. Although their hermeneutical and interpretive principles were different from the early church fathers, and New Testament authors, they all agreed on biblical authority. Both of these groups believed, that what was contained in the Scriptures, was consistent and homogenous, and that there were no contradictions in the Scripture. Scripture was seen as the Word of God in the way it represented verbal cognitive revelation. The very idea of progressive revelation, they considered impossible, if this meant that a "complete and saving revelation" was not given to Moses. In early Judaism, there was a complete "correspondence and agreement" between Moses, the prophetic books, and the Hagiographa (the Writings), which explains the Pentateuch, the same as for early Christians the New Testament "explained" the Old Testament. The New Testament writers, as well as Jesus Himself, regarded the Old Testament very much the same as the Jews did, but they interpreted it "Christologically", as did the early church during apostolic times. The early Christian fathers, the apostolic fathers, and the apologists, held to the fact of the Old Testament being inspired by God, and of being authorized of God, many years before the New Testament was canonized. The Old Testament was used as divine authority in the proclamation of Christ's gospel. It was considered in those days, as a Christian book, because it witnessed of Jesus Christ, as referred to in 1 Peter 1: 10-12. The early apologists came to faith in Jesus Christ, by reading the Old Testament, along with the personal witness of Christ's apostles. After the time of the early apologists, the New Testament writings were accepted, along with the Old Testament, and both were considered together, as having divine authority. They were both, as one complete unit, seen to be the divinely authorized Word of God. The New Testament was, in a sense, the "divinely authoritative commentary" on the Old Testament.[71] All the early church fathers considered the Scriptures to be the Word of God, because of their divine origin. This belief, was not from ancient Judaism, but came directly from the New Testament, as it says in 2 Timothy 3: 16 that Scripture was "God-breathed". The writers of the New Testament were seen, as "instruments of the Holy Spirit" (2 Peter 1: 21). The early church fathers, accepted that Scripture was God's Word, and treated it accordingly; much like the New Testament writers had viewed the Old Testament Scriptures. These men believed that God Himself was the actual author of the Scriptures.[72] God inspired the Holy Scriptures. Revelation is distinguished from inspiration, in that revelation is the message, and inspiration was God's method, in delivering that message to mankind. The Holy Spirit through inspiration, revealed to human writers the particular message God wanted to be included, in the Old and New Testaments.[73]

The International Council on Biblical Inerrancy set forth the divine inspiration of Scripture the following way: "God, who is Himself Truth and Speaks Truth only, has inspired Holy Scripture in order to reveal Himself to lost mankind through Jesus Christ as Creator and Lord, Redeemer and Judge. Holy Scripture is God's witness to Himself. Holy Scripture...is to be 1. Believed, as God's instruction, in all that it affirms; 2. Obeyed, as God's command, in all that is required; 3. Embraced, as God's pledge, in all that it promises. The doctrine of inerrancy has been integral to the Church's faith throughout its history. A confession of the full authority, infallibility, and inerrancy of Scripture is vital to a sound understanding of the whole of the Christian faith...such confession should lead to increasing conforming to the image of Christ."[74]

Jesus warns us in Matthew 5: 19 by stating, "Whoever then relaxes one of the least of these commandments and teaches men so shall be called least in the kingdom of heaven." It is clear and obvious that God does not want anyone changing His Word. In all actuality, His Word cannot be changed. It states in Luke 16: 17 "It is easier for heaven and earth to pass away than for one stroke of a letter of the Law to fail." Men would try to change God's Word. Jesus Himself told the Pharisees, they had "invalidated" His Word by their tradition (Mark 7: 13). Through their manmade traditions, and false interpretations, they had polluted the effectiveness of His Word. They had ignored parts of His Word, which in turn was like ignoring all of His Word, because the Scripture was a "unit", not meant to be broken. It says in Psalm 119: 60, "Thy Word is true from the beginning; and every one of Thy righteous judgments endures forever. The Bible is "infallible", and speaks only the truth. God is perfect, and so is His Word. It says in Psalm 19: 7, "The Law of the Lord is perfect."[75] God has warned us about tampering with His Word. Proverbs 30: 6 states, "Do not add to His Words lest he reprove you, and you be proved a liar." If anyone claims to have new revelations or new inspiration from God, Revelation 22: 18-19 describes the outcome: "I warn everyone who hears the words of the prophecy of this book: if anyone adds to them, God will add to him the plagues described in this book, and if anyone takes away from the words of the book of this prophecy, God will take away his share in the tree of life and in the holy city, which are described in this book."[76] There is no more revelation needed. Scripture is complete, and the Bible is all that we need for a right relationship with God. There is no need for a new vision, revelation, or voice from heaven. The New Testament authors were either apostles, or those close to the apostles, and they were, as is stated in Ephesians 2: 20, the "foundation" of the church. There are no more apostles on the earth today, so there are no more revelations. The foundation of the church has been established, on the witness of Jesus Christ by the apostles, and no other foundation is being re-laid. Today it could be said, that we have "illumination of Scripture" by the Holy Spirit, not by God inspiring men to write more of His Word. God's Word carries His authority. It is stated in Isaiah 1: 2, "Hear, O heavens, and give ear, O earth; for the Lord has spoken." God's voice is in Scripture, and that is where we turn to hear His Word. The Bible, which is made up of the Old and New Testament, is sufficient. It states in 2 Timothy 3: 16-17, "All

Scripture is inspired by God and profitable for teaching, for reproof, for correction, for training in righteousness; that the man of God may be adequate, equipped for every good work." Nothing has been left out of the Bible. It is all anyone needs to come to salvation, and become a fully equipped and mature believer. It can be said, that the Bible is "infallible, inerrant, complete, authoritative, and sufficient." It is also very much able. Hebrews 4: 12 states "For the Word of God is living and active and sharper than any two-edged sword, and piercing as far as the division of soul and spirit, of both joints and marrow, and able to judge the thoughts and intentions of the heart." God has also said about His Word in Isaiah 55: 11, "So shall My Word be which goes forth from My mouth; it shall not return to Me empty, without accomplishing what I desire and without succeeding in the matter for which I sent it." In 1 Thessalonians 1: 5, Paul reminded the Thessalonians, "For our Gospel did not come to you in Word only, but also in power and in Holy Spirit and with full conviction." The Bible is a powerful book, which can in a sense, tear a person up and put them back together again. The Word of God, along with the Spirit of God, is like "dynamite".[77] The Bible can be spoken of as a "mirror", rather than a photograph.[78]

God's Word can heal us. It has been stated, "Our natural tendency is to run from someone who knows too much about us. But because God knows everything there is to know about us, there is no place to hide. But God does not leave us on the operating table unattended. Through His Word He shows us what He sees, not that we might run from Him, but that we might run to Him. He wants us to flee to His grace and forgiveness."[79]

CHAPTER 2: PROPHETS AND PROPHECY

Prophecy is the foretelling of events, that only God could know about, through His omniscience. The biblical standard for a true prophet is one hundred percent accuracy in his predictions. There have always existed both true prophets of God, and false prophets. True prophets of the Old Testament, had a message from God to deliver to the people. These men proclaimed the will of God. They often called people to repentance. They spoke of the future coming of that last great sacrifice, Jesus Christ. When Jesus came, He came to initiate the fulfillment of His threefold responsibility of being Prophet, Priest, and King. There exists a distinction between Old Testament prophets who "foretold", and New Testament prophets who "forth-tell". There is no longer a need today of a prophet who foretells, as existed in Old Testament times.

Prophecy is predicting specific events in the future, which are only known by God, and not by man. Prophecy is more than a "good guess", or mere "conjecture". In all reality, prophecy is the "statement of historical fact that is known only to God."[80] God sets forth in His Word, the standard for prophecy. It states in Deuteronomy 18: 20, "But the prophet, which shall presume to speak a word in My name, which I have not commanded him to speak, or that shall speak in the name of other gods, even that prophet shall die." God told us in His Word, that He has no tolerance for false prophets. Deuteronomy 18: 21-22 states "And if thou say in thine heart, How shall we know the word which the Lord has not spoken? When a prophet speaks in the name of the Lord, if the thing follow not, nor come to pass, that is the thing which the Lord has not spoken but the prophet hath spoken it presumptuously; thou shalt not be afraid of him." There was a standard for a true prophet of God. This standard was "absolute" accuracy in prediction. If, therefore one could not find one prophecy in the Bible that did not occur, then by God's standard, the Bible could be seen as false and not reliable.[81]

Certain tests can be applied to prophecies to determine their truthfulness. It may be asked, whether the prophecy was far enough removed in time from the event occurring, to have cancelled out the possibility of a man making a good guess about something, based on what he might already understand. Many people may be able to "forecast" certain events, because of how they may be following the current events of the day. A forecast however, is not true prophecy. The language of a prophecy should be examined to determine, whether or not it is ambiguous, and could possibly have various explanations. True prophecy must be "unambiguous". Isaiah in Isaiah 43: 28-45: 7, prophesied of Cyrus the King of Persia, 150 years before Cyrus actually came to power. Isaiah's language was unambiguous, in that he prophesied of Cyrus, using his actual name, as the Spirit of God directed him to do so.[82]

The prophets of the Old Testament were men, who often were powerful and influential leaders, of political, religious and social life of the nation of Israel. These men brought messages from God. There are three different Hebrew words that can be translated as prophet. Two of these words come from the verbs "Ro'eh" and "Chozeh". Ro'eh is used eleven times, and chozeh is used twenty-two times, in the Old Testament. These verbs convey the idea "to see", illustrating the idea that a prophet is a man who "sees". A prophet may be called a "seer". He is able to see things of God, in a way that others cannot. The third Hebrew word that can be translated as prophet is "Nabhi". This word is used three hundred times in the Old Testament. It means to "announce" or to "bubble up". A prophet "announces" to the people, what God wants them to know. A prophet then, is a man who sees what others cannot see, as God opens his eyes to truth, and then declares or speaks his message to the people.[83]

The Old Testament prophets of Israel prophesied for God, over many centuries. Especially from the time of the Judges to Malachi, they spoke for God to the Israelite people. There was more prophecy during the time of the kings, particularly during the last years of the kingdoms of Israel and Judah, than at any other Old Testament period. The course of Hebrew history was strongly influenced by these prophets.[84]

When studying the prophets of the Old Testament, certain common characteristics emerge. They were both "influenced" and "motivated", by being called by God, to speak to the people. They were well aware of God's authority, and because of this, were able to announce God's message, both "courageously" and "uncompromisingly". They were men, who were often "solitary", and spent much time alone in communion with God. They were very individualistic men, who were free from the traditions and customs of the day. They were fearless opponents of evil practice, by individuals or the entire nation of Israel. Many of them prophesied of Israel's future as a nation, and of the Kingdom of God.[85]

There are sixteen books of prophecy in the Old Testament. These are divided into the "major" and "minor" prophets. There are four major prophetic books, and twelve minor prophetic books. These designations refer to the length of the books, and not to the value of the books.[86]

These Old Testament prophets were servants of God. They were preachers who preached the righteousness of God. They had a mission to tell the people of their time what God wanted the people to hear. They set forth God's will for the people. They often called the people to repentance. They gave the people more knowledge of God, and what God wanted the people to know about and to understand.[87]

One crucial fact, that cannot be ignored, is the relationship between the prophets of the Old Testament, and the work of Jesus Christ. It states poignantly in Hebrews 1: 1-2 "God, who at sundry times and in divers manners spake in time past unto the fathers by the prophets, hath in these last days spoken unto us by His Son, whom he hath appointed heir of all things, by whom also he made the worlds" For more than a thousand years, God spoke through His prophets, until the later days when He, Himself, became the message. He came Himself, and brought reconciliation of all the "partial and fragmentary" utterances of the prophets. His prophets had prophesied for many years about His coming, and He came Himself, as the "one supreme and final revelation of God."[88]

Moses predicted that God would raise up a prophet like himself. He stated in Deuteronomy 18: 15 "The Lord thy God will raise up unto thee a Prophet from the midst of thee, of thy brethren, like unto me; unto him ye shall hearken." The ultimate fulfillment of this prophecy was Jesus Christ, who was identified as that prophet, in Acts 3: 22-24. These verses state "For Moses truly said unto the fathers, A prophet shall the

Lord your God raise up unto you of your brethren, like unto me; him shall ye hear in all things whatsoever he shall say unto you. And it shall come to pass, that every soul, which will not hear that prophet, shall be destroyed from among the people." The everyday people of Christ's day, esteemed Him as a prophet, to the extent that the Pharisees and chief priests, were afraid to take definite action against Him (Matt. 21: 11, 46; Jn. 7: 40-43). Jesus Himself claimed to be a prophet (Matt. 13: 57; Mark 6: 4; Luke 4: 24; 13: 33; Jn. 4: 44). He claimed that He came to deliver God's message to mankind (John 8: 26; 12: 49-50; 15: 15; 17: 8).[89]

The prophetic ministry of Jesus Christ was "authenticated" in two ways. He prophesied accurately about events that took place, and He performed many miracles. He correctly predicted in detail His death. In Matthew 26: 21 He prophesied, that one of His close associates would betray Him. In Matthew 16: 21 He says that Jewish leaders would initiate His death. In Matthew 20: 19, He predicted that His death would be by crucifixion, and that He would be raised from the dead after three days. Certain miracles that He performed, testified to the people that He was a true prophet. Luke 7: 16 states "And there came a fear on all: and they glorified God, saying, that a great prophet is risen up among us; and That God hath visited His people." When the blind man whose sight was restored, was asked what he thought of Jesus in John 9: 17, He stated "He is a prophet."[90] It can be said that Christ functioned as a prophet in the Old Testament, and then continued this work as a prophet, while He was on earth.[91] A prophet often brought together three ways of satisfying his prophetic office – "teaching, predicting, and miracle-working." Jesus did all these while He was on the earth.[92]

Jesus Christ is a Prophet, and He alone is "supreme and final in that office." He alone, fulfilled every mandate of the office of a Prophet. Every statement that Christ made was a divine message of God.[93] It could be said, that "the prophet spoke for God to men, while the priest acted on behalf of men before God." Christ not only spoke for God to men, but He was the "living embodiment of that Word." The Israelites were looking ahead and waiting for a prophet who would come, and "sum up both the prophetic ideal and the prophetic message" ever since the time of Moses.

Christ called Himself a prophet. He completely and fully represented the "righteousness of God" that He proclaimed. He, as God, walking among men in the flesh, incarnate, brought together the "working of righteousness and grace for our salvation." He, at the same time proclaimed, and was the righteousness of God.[94]

There were four stages of the prophetic work of Jesus Christ. First, as the Logos, He brought enlightenment to mankind, before He came as Immanuel in flesh. All knowledge of God came from Jesus Christ. Second, as incarnate on the earth, He submitted, as did all the Old Testament prophets, to guidance and direction of the Holy Spirit, however He was Himself the very source of all "knowledge and power." God's Word did not come to Him as it did to other prophets of old, He was the Word Himself. The third stage of Christ's prophetic work was His guiding, and teaching of His people, while on earth, and then after His ascension. He, through the Holy Spirit, is continuing to direct and guide His church. The fourth stage of His prophetic work will be His "final revelation of the Father to His saints in glory." The prophetic work of Jesus Christ will go on forever, because it is infinite and eternal.[95]

Bible interpreters who lived in the time of the Old Testament, as well as those living in New Testament times, believed that "the title Messiah of the Old Covenant and the title Christ of the New Covenant imply a threefold official responsibility – that of Prophet, Priest, and King."[96] Jesus Christ was, and is, the "final Prophet of all prophets, the final Priest of all priests, and the final King of all kings."[97] There truly is none like Him.

New Testament prophets differ from Old Testament prophets, in that they forth tell rather than foretell. The prophetic word is final and complete, as it is as written in the Bible. All foretelling about the future is complete in the Bible. What one may read about in the Bible, completes the story until the end of God's plan. There is no longer any need for a prophet who foretells of future events. Ephesians 4: 11, referring to Christ, states "He gave some, apostles; and some, prophets; and some, evangelists; and some, pastors and teachers. An apostle only had a right to this title, based on his "immediate relation to Christ", while Christ was on earth. Apostles did not exist, after the "first generation" of the church on the earth.

A New Testament prophet fulfills the mandate as set forth in 1 Cor. 14: 3, "But he that prophesieth speaketh unto men to edification, and exhortation, and comfort." Prophecy in New Testament times is a gift of God's Spirit. It states in 1 Cor. 12: 10 "To another the working of miracles; to another prophecy; to another discerning of spirits; to another divers kinds of tongues; to another the interpretation of tongues." The church today is literally being built up, on the testimony of the apostles, as set forth in the New Testament, and upon New Testament prophets, who through the gift of prophecy, which is a gift of the Holy Spirit; speak to the truth of God's Word. Ephesians 2: 19-20 states "Now therefore ye are no more strangers and foreigners but fellow citizens with the saints, and of the household of God and are built upon the foundation of the apostles and prophets, Jesus Christ Himself being the chief cornerstone."[98]

There is great danger in heeding so-called "prophets" today; who go against what God's Word says. They are false prophets. False prophets are warned against, all throughout the New Testament. Peter warns New Testament believers in 2 Peter 2: 1, "But there were false prophets also among the people, even as there shall be false teachers among you, who privily shall bring in damnable heresies, even denying the Lord that bought them, and bring upon themselves swift destruction." Peter refers to these false prophets with the following words: presumptuous, self-willed, natural brute beasts, spots and blemishes, adulterous, cursed, wells without water, clouds carried with a tempest, speaking great words of vanity, and servants of corruption. Paul warns the Galatians of the false prophets, which have brought them "another gospel", which was one of works. He states in Galatians 1: 16 "I marvel that ye are so soon removed from him that called you into the grace of Christ unto another gospel." John warns New Testament Christians about false teachers, who lie and deny that Jesus is the Christ. It states in 1 John 2: 18 "Little children, it is the last time: and as ye have heard that antichrist shall come, even now there are many antichrists; whereby we know that it is the last time." John warns in 2 John about those, who would come denying that Christ had come in the flesh. It states in 2 John 9-10 "whosoever transgresseth, and abideth not in the doctrine of Christ, hath not God. He that abideth in the doctrine of Christ, he hath both the Father and the Son. If there come any unto you, and bring not this doctrine, receive him not into your house, neither bid him Godspeed." The entire New Testament book of Jude is a strong wake-up call to diligence; in recognizing false prophets, Jude urges believers to contend for the faith. He speaks of "certain men" who "crept in unawares", who were "ungodly men", who turned the grace of God into "lasciviousness", and denied the only Lord God. He speaks of these false teachers, or false prophets, as "filthy dreamers" who "defile the flesh", "despise dominion" and "speak evil of dignities." He refers to them as "clouds without water who are carried about by winds, as trees whose fruit withereth without fruit, being twice dead, plucked up by the roots, and as raging waves of the sea foaming out their own shame, and wandering stars to whom blackness of darkness is reserved forever. He further describes them as; murmerers, complainers, speakers of great swelling words, mockers who walk after their own ungodly lusts, and as sensual men having not the Spirit. Throughout the New Testament, false prophets are warned about. They often come as wolves in sheep's clothing, or as an angel of light, to deceive Christian believers. Following them only leads to destruction.

CHAPTER 3: PRIESTHOOD AND TEMPLES

A priest is one who offers sacrifices at the altar and acts as mediator between man and God. Priestly functions have been carried out, historically since early patriarchal times, by the heads of families. Job, Noah, and Abraham all functioned in this capacity as priests.[99] The concept of intercession between God and man Is the basis of Old Testament priesthood. God was teaching the Israelites through the Law of Moses, and the system of sacrifice established, that ultimately there would be one last great sacrifice – that of Jesus Christ. Aaron was instructed to come once a year, with a bull, a ram, and a goat, to a holy place, and sacrifice them with a "laying on of hands and sprinkling the blood of the bull and the goat on the mercy seat and offering the ram as a burnt offering." A second goat, a "scapegoat", was driven out into the wilderness, with the "laying on of hands and the confession of the sins of the people." This Mosaic system of sacrifice, was similar to what Abraham was commanded by God to do, where God provided a ram as a substitute for the sacrifice of Isaac.

In the history of sacrifice, there exists the continual theme of God interceding and providing the sacrifice. This stands in complete opposition, to the pagan idea of sacrificing to a god, where man is trying to obtain the favor of that god, with the idea being that doing so will cause a change to the god's favor by that man's sacrifice. In the Old Testament sacrifice of the Israelites, a work was done "by man in the hope of changing the heart of man, cleansing him so as to render him acceptable to God." In both the Old and New Testaments, however, the fact is that "God intercedes" and provides a sacrifice, that "changes the wrath of God into mercy and the sinner into a saint."[100] In pagan sacrifice, there is a human effort to control the gods or that god's favor, but as in Abraham's sacrifice of the ram, Abraham exercised faith, that God would provide a sacrifice.[101] In Genesis 22: 5, Abraham hinted of the faith he had when he said that both he and Isaac would return from Mount Moriah. It states, "And Abraham said unto his young men, Abide ye here with the ass; and I and the lad will go yonder and worship, and come again to you." Abraham let Isaac know what he was thinking. Genesis 22: 8 states "And Abraham said, my son, God will provide himself a lamb for a burnt offering: so they went both of them together." Abraham had faith that God would provide, while being obedient to the test that God placed before him. This became a beautiful example of how God would provide a sacrifice, in sending His only begotten Son, as complete fulfillment of the system of sacrifice that had been established by the Law of Moses.

Christ is a High Priest, after the order of Melchizedec. Speaking of Christ, Psalm 110: 4 states, "The Lord hath sworn, and will not repent, Thou art a priest forever after the order of Melchizedec." This priesthood was distinct, from the Israelite priesthood set up by Moses. Exodus 28: 1 states, "And take thou unto thee Aaron thy brother, and his sons with him, from among the children of Israel, that he may minister unto me in the priest's office, even Aaron, Nadab and Abihu,

Eleazar and Ithamar, Aaron's sons." The Israelite priesthood included three basic classes: the high priest, the priests, and the Levites. The Levites served the priests, by performing functions such as physical care of the tabernacle, and as musicians and treasurers.[102] Priests were consecrated publicly at the age of thirty, as prescribed by the Law of Moses. (Numbers 4: 3)[103]

Jesus was not a priest after the order of Aaron, but after the order of Melchizedec. As it states in Hebrews 7: 3 describing Melchizedec, and in reality describing Jesus, "Without father, without mother, without descent, having neither beginning of days, nor end of life; but made like unto the Son of God; abideth a priest continually." His priesthood did not come from being in the lineage of Levi and Aaron, but from God Himself. Christ was from the tribe of Judah, and because of this did not qualify as a priest after the order of Aaron.

John the Baptist had a mission to both, "make ready a people for the Lord" (Luke 1: 17), and "to manifest the Messiah." John the Baptist stated in John 1: 31, "But that He (Christ) should be made manifest to Israel, therefore I am come baptizing with water." John identified Him as the Lamb of God (John 1: 29), and inducted him into His public ministry (Jesus' public ministry) by baptism. This was done in order to fulfill part of the requirements of the Mosaic Law. Jesus was a priest, and as such, He needed to be consecrated. The baptism of Jesus by John, was in compliance to the required fulfillment of the Mosaic Law. Jesus, as priest, became "both the sacrificer and the sacrifice." He acted as an officiating priest, similar to the Aaronic pattern, and the actual sacrificial lamb. As it states in Hebrews 10: 12, "But this man, after he had offered one sacrifice for sins forever, sat down on the right hand of God." Jesus did not follow the Aaronic order or pattern, in offering on the Day of Atonement, a sacrifice for His own sins. He offered Himself as a sacrifice.[104]

There are "analogies and contrasts" between the priesthood of Aaron or Levi, and Christ's priesthood, after the order of Melchizedec. He was without sin, and did not need to offer up a sacrifice for Himself, as the other priests did. The blood of bulls and goats could not take away sin, only His could. Theirs could only "cover" sin, temporarily. The work that Christ did, was "once for all", whereas the work of the other priests, had to be repeated.[105]

The Melchizedec priesthood of Christ, as is described uniquely in Hebrews 7, "For this Melchizedec, King of Salem, priest of the Most High God, who met Abraham of the kings, and blessed him; To whom also Abraham gave a tenth part of all; first being by interpretation King of righteousness, and after that also King of Salem, which is, King of Peace." Melchizedec was a type of the "eternal and kingly character", of the work of Jesus Christ. His work did not have anything to do with "sprinkling animal blood in an earthly tabernacle, where the priest passed beyond the embroidered veil shielding the holiest place, but with presenting His own sacrifice in the very 'temple' of heaven, the antitype of the earthly." His "priestly order, priestly service, and sacrifice are celestial, eternal, supranational, and final."[106]

An Aaronic priest had to be someone who was chosen by God, and who qualified for this office. Hebrews 5: 1-9 sets forth the qualifications Jesus had in His priestly office and service, "For every high priest taken from among men is ordained for men in things pertaining to God, that he may offer both gifts and sacrifices for sins: who can have compassion on the ignorant, and on them that are out of the way; for that he himself also is compassed with infirmity. And by reason hereof he ought, as for the people, so also for himself, to offer for sins. And no man taketh this honour unto himself, but he that is called of God, as was Aaron. So also Christ glorified not himself to be made a high priest; but he that said unto him, Thou art my Son, today have I begotten thee. As he saith also in another place, Thou art a priest forever after the order of Melchizedec. Who in the days of his flesh, when he had offered up prayers and supplications with strong crying and tears unto him that was able to save him from death and was heard in that he feared; Though he were a Son, yet learned he obedience by the things which he suffered; and being made perfect, he became the author of eternal salvation unto all them that obey him."

The features of the Melchizedec priesthood are as follows: 1. It was a royal priesthood. Melchizedec was both a king and a priest, which was different from the priests who held the priesthood of Aaron. Speaking of Jesus, Zechariah 6: 13 states that "he shall be a priest upon his throne." 2. This priesthood had nothing to do with ancestry. Jesus did not depend on his ancestry to qualify as a priest, as did the Aaronic priests.   3. This Melchizedec priesthood of Christ was timeless, having no beginning or end. 4. This Melchizedec priesthood was superior to the priesthood of Aaron.[107] Christ's priesthood is eternal, and is "sealed as such by the oath of Jehovah."[108] It states in Hebrews 7: 20-28, "And inasmuch as not without an oath he was made priest: (For those priests were made without an oath; but this with an oath by him that said unto him, The Lord sware and will not repent, Thou art a priest forever after the order of Melchizedec) By so much was Jesus made a surety of a better testament. And they truly were many priests, because they were not suffered to continue by reason of death: But this man, because he continueth forever, hath an unchangeable priesthood. Wherefore he is able also to save them to the uttermost that come unto God by him, seeing he ever liveth to make intercession for them. For such an high priest became us, who is holy, harmless, undefiled, separate from sinners, and made higher than the heavens; who needeth not daily, as those high priests, to offer up sacrifice, first for his own sins, and then for the peoples': for this he did once, when he offered up himself. For the law maketh men high priests which have infirmity; but the word of the oath, which was since the law, maketh the Son, who is consecrated for evermore." Christ, as a perfect man, offered Himself as a "fragrant offering and sacrifice to God." It states in 2 Cor. 5: 21, "For He hath made Him to be sin for us, who knew no sin; that we might be made the righteousness of God in Him." This intercession needed to be made by one who could represent both sides. When man, as priest, was offering a sacrifice, the sacrifice was never truly spotless. In the intercession of Jesus Christ, a truly pure and sinless gift was given.[109] The sacrifice of Jesus, does not "buy" divine love, but it is the gift of His love for us, in that He submits to the judgment of our sin. We were all subject to death through Adam's transgression, and Jesus entered into our judgment of death. His atoning act "is His High priesthood, where He joins Himself to us and makes reconciliation for sin, and, now having entered into heaven, He continues His intercessory ministry for us." He, as it has been written, "bore our judgment and He died our death; He carried our sorrows and He lives now to succor us."[110]

As a result of Christ's resurrection, He has become our high Priest. He has become the "intercessor, executive, and protector" of His people. It states in Romans 8: 34, "Who is he that condemneth? It is Christ that died, yea rather, that is risen again, who is even at the right hand of God, who also maketh intercession for us."[111]

Priests, throughout the Old Testament, had the special privilege of "approach to God, and of speaking and acting in behalf of the people."

It states in 1 Timothy 2: 5, "For there is one God, and one mediator between God and men, the man Christ Jesus." Christ is now our great high Priest, and makes intercession for us. Ephesians 1: 16-23 states, "The eyes of your understanding being enlightened; that ye may know what is the hope of his calling, and what the riches of the glory of his inheritance in the saints, and what is the exceeding greatness of his power to us-ward who believe, according to the working of His mighty power, which he wrought in Christ, when he raised him from the dead, and set Him at His own right hand in the heavenly places, far above all principality, and power, and might, and dominion, and every name that is named, not only in this world, but also in that which is to come: and hath put all things under His feet, and gave Him to be the head over all things to the church, which is his body, the fullness of him that filleth all in all."

Christ Is called our "parakletos", which means advocate, comforter, or consoler. It states in 1 John 2: 1, "My little children, these things write I unto you, that ye sin not. And if any man sin, we have an advocate with the Father, Jesus Christ the Righteous." "His intercessory work is based on His sacrifice, and is not limited, as is sometimes thought, to intercessory prayer. He presents His sacrifice to God, and on the grounds of it, claims all spiritual blessings for His people, defends them against the charges of Satan, the law, and conscience, secures forgiveness for everything justly charged against them, and sanctifies their worship and service through the operation of the Holy Spirit."[112]

The priestly work of Christ was not limited to His sacrificial offering of Himself on the cross; He is today a heavenly High Priest. He is today a minister of the sanctuary, of the true tabernacle, which the Lord pitched, and not man (Hebrews 8: 2). He began His work as priest on the earth, and is continuing it in heaven. He is not counted among earthly priests, because they were only a "shadow" of a coming reality. He is the "real Priest", serving at the "real sanctuary" in heaven.[113]

In the Old Testament, the most important or crucial part of sacrifice, was not in the slaying of the victim, but in what was done with the blood of the victim, when it was released. The blood meant the life of the victim. On the Day of Atonement, the high Priest would enter into the holy of holies, behind the veil of the temple, and would sprinkle the mercy seat with the blood of the animal that had been sanctified. The moment of the pouring out of Christ's blood, is not only at Golgotha, but also in the presentation of His sacrifice to the Father at His ascension. The continual intercession Christ is making for us is equivalent to what the Old Testament high Priest did, with the blood of the sacrifice, when he entered into the Holy of Holies. It states in Hebrews 7: 25, "Wherefore He is able also to save them to the uttermost that come unto God by Him, seeing He ever liveth to make intercession for them." Jesus does not offer Himself repeatedly, as the earthly high priest did, but He appeared once for all. It states in Hebrews 9: 24-25, "For Christ is not entered into the holy places made with hands, which are the figures of the true; but into heaven itself, now to appear in the presence of God for us: Nor yet that He should offer Himself often, as the high Priest entereth into the holy place every year with blood of others." He lives now in the heavenly Holy of Holies, to make intercession for us.

Through Christ's intercession, His priestly office is combined with His kingly office. Hebrews 10: 12-13 states, "But this man, after he had offered one sacrifice for sins forever, sat down on the right hand of God; From henceforth expecting till His enemies be made His footstool." Jesus was exalted after His resurrection, and sits at the right hand of the Father, and rules over heaven and earth. His kingly work is the continuous intercession before God on our behalf. God's glory is Christ's intercessory work.[114]

As He does this work on our behalf, the Holy Spirit calls, and gathers the church. Christ is operating in the world today, through His Holy Spirit, drawing all men to Himself. "The biblical proclamation of Christ's intercessory work, teaches that the glorious suffering of Christ draws us, into a participating fellowship, in which peace is made with God, and new life is given to His fallen creatures, so that they in turn may glorify God through a joyful suffering in this world."[115]

Believers in Jesus Christ form a royal priesthood. 1 Peter 2: 5 states, "Ye also, as lively stones, are built up a spiritual house, an holy priesthood, to offer up spiritual sacrifices, acceptable to God by Jesus Christ." We derive all our positions and possessions from Christ. It states in Revelation 1: 5-6, "And from Jesus Christ, who is the faithful witness, and the first begotten of the dead, and the Prince of the kings of the earth. Unto Him that loved us, and washed us from our sins in His own blood, and hath made us kings and priests unto God and His Father; to Him be glory and dominion forever and ever. Amen."

When we become children of God by accepting Jesus Christ, we become priests, because of our relationship to Christ, our great High Priest. We shall reign with Christ on the earth, during His millennial reign. It states in Revelation 5: 10, "And hast made us unto our God kings and priests: and we shall reign on the earth." Every "saved" or born again believer in this present age is a priest unto God. "The Old Testament priest is a type of the New Testament priest. Israel had a priesthood; the Church is a priesthood."[116]

Just as there was a high Priest over Israel's priesthood, Jesus Christ is High Priest over the church. Hebrews 4: 14-16 describes the relationship that we can have with Jesus, our High Priest, "Seeing then that we have a great High Priest, that is passed into the heavens, Jesus the Son of God, let us hold fast our profession. For we have not an high priest which cannot be touched with the feeling of our infirmities; but was in all points tempted like as we are, yet without sin. Let us therefore come boldly unto the throne of grace that we may obtain mercy, and find grace to help in time of need."

The doctrine of the New Testament priesthood was explained by Dr. C.I. Scofield in the following way: "1. Until the law was given, the head of each family was the family priest (Gen. 8: 20; 26: 25; 31: 54). 2. When the law was proposed, the promise to perfect obedience was that Israel should be unto God 'a kingdom of priests' (Exodus 19: 6); but Israel violated the law, and God shut up the priestly office to the Aaronic family, appointing the tribe of Levi: to minister to them, thus constituting the typical priesthood (Exodus 28: 1). 3. In the dispensation of grace, all believers are unconditionally constituted a 'kingdom of priests' (1 Peter 2: 9; Rev. 1: 6), the distinction which Israel failed to achieve by works. The priesthood of the believer is, therefore, a birthright; just as every descendant of Aaron was born to the priesthood (Heb. 5: 1). 4. The chief privilege of a priest is access to God. Under law, only the high priest could enter 'the holiest of all' and that but once a year (Heb. 9: 7). But when Christ died, the veil, a type of Christ's human body (Heb. 10: 20), was rent, so that now the believer – priests, equally with Christ the High Priest, have access to God in the holiest (Heb. 10: 19-22). The High Priest is corporally there (4: 14-16; Heb. 9: 24; 10: 19-22). 5. In the exercise of his office the New Testament believer – priest is 1. A sacrificer who offers a threefold sacrifice: a. his own living body

(Rom. 12: 1; Phil. 2: 17; 2 Tim. 4: 6; 1 John 3: 16; Jas 1: 27); b. praise to God, "the fruit of the lips that make mention of His name", to be offered 'continually' (Heb. 13: 15; Ex. 25: 22; 'I will commune with thee from above the mercy seat'); c. his substance (Heb. 13: 16; Rom. 12: 13; Gal. 6: 6; 3 John 5-8; Heb. 13: 2; Gal. 6: 10; Tit. 3: 14). 2. The New Testament priest is also an intercessor (1 Tim. 2: 1; Col. 4: 12)."[117]

A sanctuary in the Old Testament was a special place set apart for the Lord's presence to dwell among His people.[118] The tabernacle of Moses in the wilderness, and the temples of Solomon, Zerubbabel and Herod were all places where the Israelites, through the priests, performed ritual sacrifices in fulfillment of the Law of Moses. A temple was considered a "house" or dwelling place of God. The temples of Solomon, Zerubbabel and Herod, which were all subsequently destroyed, were national sanctuaries of the Jews, which were located in Jerusalem, each in their time, on Mount Moriah. This was the site where Abraham took Isaac to be sacrificed, in obedience to God's command. In the Holy of Holies of these temples, was found the Ark of the Covenant, with its' top being called the mercy seat. It was here where God manifested His Shekinah glory.[119] The word Shekinah is alluding to the visible presence of God, which was associated with light.[120] It states in Exodus 40: 34, "Then a cloud covered the tent of the congregation, and the glory of the Lord filled the tabernacle."

The tabernacle relates in a symbolic way to Jesus Christ. This fact is "significant" in the following ways: "1. It was a portrayal of a heavenly reality (Heb. 9: 23-24). 2. The tabernacle was typical of the church, which is 'a habitation of God through the Spirit' (Ex. 25: 9; Eph. 2: 19-22). 3. The tabernacle was typical of the individual believer who is 'a temple of the Holy Spirit' (1 Cor. 6: 19; 2 Cor. 6: 16). 4. The holiness of

God was vividly portrayed in the tabernacle...5. The tabernacle at the same time was a demonstration of the grace of God...6. The chief significance of the tabernacle belongs to the theology of the incarnation. In the New Testament, the idea of the divine presence culminates in the person of Jesus Christ, in whom 'the Word was made flesh, and dwelt (lit. tabernacled) among us' (John 1: 14), and in whom 'all the fullness of God was pleased to dwell' (Col. 1: 19; 2: 9)"[121]

The furniture which was in the Holy of Holies, represented God's approach to man, not man's approach to God. It was here, that the "holiness, grace, and sovereignty" of God, were shown, in what God Himself provided for us. Jesus Christ as our High Priest "took the blood of His sacrifice and sprinkled it over the broken law that we might be regarded as perfect in God's eyes (Heb. 9: 11-15; 10: 19)."[122] Hebrews 9: 11-16 states "But Christ being come an high priest of good things to come, by a greater and more perfect tabernacle not made with hands, that is to say, not of this building; Neither by the blood of goats and calves, but by his own blood he entered in once into the holy place, having obtained eternal redemption for us. For if the blood of bulls and goats, and the ashes of an heifer sprinkling the unclean, sanctifieth to the purifying of the flesh: How much more shall the blood of Christ, who through the eternal spirit offered himself without spot to God, purge your conscience from dead works to serve the living God? And for this cause he is the mediator of the New Testament that by means of death, for the redemption of the transgressions that were under the first testament, they which are called might receive the promise of eternal inheritance. For where a testament is, there must also of necessity be the death of the testator." The furniture in the Holy of Holies, such as the table of showbread, was symbolic of Jesus being the bread of life. The golden lampstand, signified how He was the light of the world, as well as the light "who lights every man who comes into the world" (Jn. 1: 9), in that He is God's "final and ultimate" revelation. It states in Hebrews 1: 1-3, "God, who at sundry times and in divers manners spake in time past unto the fathers by the prophets, hath in these last days spoken unto us by his Son, whom he hath appointed heir of all things, by whom also he made the worlds; who being the brightness of his glory, and the express image of his person, and upholding all things by the word of his power, when he had by himself purged our sins, sat down on the right hand of the Majesty on high." The altar of incense represented Jesus as our Intercessor. Hebrews 7: 25 states "Wherefore he is able also to save them to the uttermost that come unto God by him, seeing he ever liveth to make intercession for them."[123]

It states in 1 John 1: 5 "Then this is the message which we have heard of him, and declare unto you, that God is light, and in him is no darkness at all." God is light. It states in 1 Tim. 6: 16, "Who only hath immortality, dwelling in the light which no man can approach unto; whom no man hath seen, nor can see: to whom be honor and power everlasting. Amen." God dwells in light.[124] People never went to the tabernacle, or to the temple to see God. God's glory, His Shekinah glory, was manifested to the people.

The beginning of the book of Exodus relates to Moses seeing God's glory in the burning bush, and at the end of Exodus the glory of God is manifested in the tabernacle.[125] Solomon during his dedicatory prayer he prayed after the temple was built expressed the insignificance of the edifice when compared to God's greatness. 2 Chronicles 6: 18 states "But will God in very deed dwell with men on the earth? Behold, heaven and the heaven of heavens cannot contain thee; how much less this house which I have built." Solomon realized that God was Spirit, and could not be "contained" in an earthly building.[126] God expresses His immensity, as it states in Isaiah 66: 1, "Thus saith the Lord, The heaven is my throne, and the earth is my footstool: where is the house that ye build unto me? And where is the place of my rest?"

To the Israelites, the tabernacle and temples functioned as a place where God manifested His glory to them. Through the tabernacles and temples, they were able to fulfill the sacrificial requirements of the Law of Moses. Ultimately, however, all was leading to the future occurrence when God would literally manifest Himself "in flesh", through His incarnation. In fulfillment of prophecy, in the meridian of time, God sent His only begotten Son. Herod's temple was the one standing in Jerusalem, during the time Jesus was on the earth.

Jesus referred to Himself in comparison to the temple in Matthew 12: 6, "But I say unto you, that in this place is one greater than the temple." Jesus was beginning to introduce a concept to the religious Jews, that a new way of coming to God was being established. John 2: 19-21 states "Jesus answered and said unto them, destroy this temple, and in three days I will raise it up. Then said the Jews, Forty and six years was this temple in building, and wilt thou rear it up in three days? But he spake of the temple of his body." Much of the Jewish faith was centered in the temple. Jesus was introducing a radical idea which most Jews, in their spiritual blindness, could not understand. If his body was the temple, the ramifications were that there would be no more need for a building. Jesus was the new sacrifice and the new temple also. Old things were being done away, and all things were becoming new.

Jesus' encounter with the Samaritan woman at the well illustrates this point. John 4: 19-24 states "The woman saith unto him, Sir, I perceive that thou art a prophet. Our fathers worshipped in this mountain; and ye say, that in Jerusalem is the place where men ought to worship. Jesus saith unto her, 'Woman believe me, the hour cometh, when ye shall neither in this mountain, nor yet at Jerusalem, worship the Father. Ye worship ye know not what: we know what we worship: for salvation is of the Jews. But the hour cometh, and now is, when the true worshippers shall worship the Father in spirit and in truth: for the Father seeketh such to worship him. God is a Spirit: and they that worship him must worship him in spirit and in truth." Jesus then, in verse 26, identifies Himself, as the Christ. John 4: 25-26 states, "The woman saith unto him, I know that Messias cometh, which is called Christ: when he is come, he will tell us all things. Jesus saith unto her, I that speak unto thee am he. Jesus truly was telling the woman at the well new things. This new worship Jesus spoke of did not have to do with "outward geography" but with "inward integrity".[127]

A very significant occurrence took place immediately following Jesus' death. Mark 15: 37-38 reads "And Jesus cried with a loud voice, and gave up the ghost. And the veil of the temple was rent in twain from the top to the bottom." The veil of the temple was a thick embroidered curtain, which separated the holy of holies from the holy place of the temple. The function of the veil was to "veil" the "immediate presence of God from the officiating priest." Only once a year, on the Day of Atonement, could the high priest go within the veil, to sprinkle blood on the mercy seat. When Jesus died, the veil was rent or torn from top to bottom, which exposed the most holy place. Jesus, as our High Priest, had entered "within the veil". Hebrews 6: 19-20 reads "Which hope we have as an anchor of the soul, both sure and steadfast, and which entereth into that within the veil; whither the forerunner is for us entered, even Jesus, made an high priest forever after the order of Melchizedec."

Now, we may also enter that holy place, through the blood of Jesus. Hebrews 10: 19-20 states "Having therefore, brethren, boldness to enter into the holiest by the blood of Jesus, By a new and living way, which he hath consecrated for us, through the veil, that is to say, his flesh." Jesus states in John 14: 6, "...I am the way, the truth, and the life: no man cometh unto the Father, but by me." The same way that the body of Jesus was torn on the cross, the veil between God and mankind was torn.[128]

It should be pointed out, that most ancient religions had their temples, pagan temples. These often had the specific idol or image of the god that they worshipped located in the inner chambers.[129] The Babylonians, Egyptians, and Canaanites all had temples.[130] These pagan cultures also had pagan priesthoods to serve in their pagan temples.[131]

As Paul took the simple but profound message, that God had come down to man as Jesus, and sacrificed Himself for us, into a "religious" pagan gentile world, he taught them something radical. As he stood "in the midst of Mars Hill" in Athens, he stated in Acts 17: 22-25, "Ye men of Athens, I perceive that in all things ye are too superstitious. For as I passed by, and beheld your devotions, I found an altar with this inscription, TO THE UNKNOWN GOD, whom therefore ye ignorantly worship, him declare I unto you. God that made the world and all things therein, seeing that he is Lord of heaven and earth, dwelleth not in temples made with hands. Neither is worshipped with men's hands, as though he needed anything, seeing he giveth to all life, and breath, and all things." Paul was introducing to the gentile world, the new idea that the true and living God is not worshipped by going to any temple. Paul introduced to the Corinthians in 1 Corinthians 3: 16 the new reality, that our bodies are temples of God. It reads "know ye not that ye are the temple of God, and that the Spirit of God dwelleth in you? It states in Galatians 4: 6, "And because ye are sons, God hath sent forth the Spirit of his Son into your hearts, crying Abba, Father." Paul further taught the young Christian believers at Corinth, "And what agreement hath the temple of God with idols? For ye are the temple of the living God; as God hath said, I will dwell in them, and walk in them; and I will be their God, and they shall be my people" (2 Cor. 6: 16). This radical concept, whether preached to Jews or Gentiles, did away with totally, the idea that God was dwelling in a temple somewhere. God was now dwelling in men's hearts, as they came to trust Jesus as their personal Savior, and ask that He forgive them and save them. There was no longer a need for any physical temple of God, after Jesus died and rose again. Today, there is still no need for a temple made with hands. It states in Ephesians 2: 12-22, "That at that time ye were without Christ, being aliens from the commonwealth of Israel, and strangers from the covenants of promise, having no hope, and without God in the world: But now in Christ Jesus ye who sometimes were far off are made nigh by the blood of Christ. For he is our peace, who hath made both one, and hath broken down the middle wall of partition between us; Having abolished in his flesh the enmity, even the law of commandments contained in ordinances; for to make in himself of twain one new man, so making peace; And that he might reconcile both unto God in one body by the cross, having slain the enmity thereby: And came and preached peace to you which were afar off, and to them that were nigh. For through him we both have access by one Spirit unto the Father. Now therefore ye are no more strangers and foreigners, but fellow citizens with the saints, and of the household of God; And are built upon the foundation of the apostles and prophets, Jesus Christ Himself being the chief cornerstone; In whom all the building fitly framed together groweth unto an holy temple in the Lord: In whom ye also are builded together for a habitation of God through the Spirit."

CHAPTER 4: THE GOD OF THE BIBLE AND THE TRINITY

John 4: 24 states, "God is a Spirit: and they that worship Him must worship Him in spirit and in truth." Here, Jesus identifies for us what God's nature is – He is a Spirit. Jesus tells us more about a spirit in Luke 24: 39, "Behold my hands and my feet, that it is I myself: handle me, and see; for a spirit hath not flesh and bones, as ye see me have. Jesus was teaching us, that a spirit does not have a body of flesh and bones. God the Father does not have a body of flesh and bones. God is a living God, but He is spirit. Joshua referred to Him in Joshua 3: 10 by saying, "Hereby ye shall know that the living God is among you…" Psalm 84: 2 also refers to a living God, "My soul longeth, yea, even fainteth for the courts of the Lord: my heart and my flesh crieth out for the living God." God is also a personal God.[132] God has self-consciousness, as it speaks of this in Exodus 3: 14, "And God said unto Moses, I AM THAT I AM: and he said, Thus shalt thou say unto the children of Israel, I AM hath sent me unto you." He also establishes His singularity in Isaiah 45: 5, "I am the Lord, and there is none else, there is no God beside me." God has self- determination. Job 23: 13 speaks of this, "But He is in one mind, and who can turn Him? And what His soul desireth, even that He doeth." In Ephesians 1: 9, God's will is spoken of – "Having made known unto us the mystery of his will, according to his good pleasure which he has purposed in Himself."

God possesses the psychological characteristics of personality, such as intellect, as is shown in Acts 15: 18, "Known unto God are all his works from the beginning of the world." He has sensitivity and feelings. Genesis 6: 6 says, "And it repented the Lord that he had made man on the earth, and it grieved him at his heart." God has volition and exercises his will. This was expressed in the garden, when God said in Genesis 3: 15 "And I will put enmity between thee and the woman, and between thy seed and her seed; it shall bruise thy head, and thou shalt bruise his heel." God can see. In Genesis 11: 5 it states, "And the Lord came down to see the city and the tower, which the children of men builded." He can also hear. Psalm 94: 9 states "he that planted the ear, shall he not hear? he that formed the eye, shall he not see?" The Bible also teaches us, that God can be angry, jealous, and compassionate. Deuteronomy 1: 37 says "Also the Lord was angry with me for your sakes...". Exodus 20: 5 states "Thou shalt not bow down thyself to them, nor serve them: for I the Lord thy God am a jealous God...". Psalm 111: 4 says "...the Lord is gracious and full of compassion."[133]

God is the creator, upholder, ruler, and sustainer of all things. Acts 14: 15 identifies Him as the "living God, which made heaven and earth, and the sea, and all things that are therein." Nehemiah 9: 6 recognizes God as the "preserver" of all His creations. It states "Thou, even thou, art Lord alone; thou hast made heaven, the heaven of heavens, with all their host, the earth, and all things that are therein, and thou preservest them all; and the host of heaven worship thee." God rules, as it states in Psalm 75: 7, "But God is the judge: he putteth down one, and setteth up another." God is our sustainer, as is spoken of in Psalm 104: 29, "Thou hidest thy face, they are troubled: thou takest away their breath, they die, and return to their dust."[134]

God is self-existent. "While man's ground of existence is outside of himself, God's existence is not dependent upon anything outside of Himself."[135] He exists in Himself, and of Himself. He owes His being to no one. His substance is not divisible, and is single in His unitary being.[136] God has the ground of His existence, in Himself. He is not self-caused or self-originated, because He is without beginning or end.[137] This truth is set forth in John 8: 58, "...Verily, verily, I say unto you, Before Abraham was, I am."

"God is infinite in relation to space. He is not limited or circumscribed by space; on the contrary, all finite space is dependent upon Him. He is, in fact, above space."[138] Solomon spoke of the immensity of God in 1 Kings 8: 27, "But will God indeed dwell on the earth? Behold, the heaven and heaven of heavens cannot contain thee; how much less this house that I have builded?" "God is both immanent and transcendent, and He is everywhere presence in essence as well as in knowledge and power."[139] David understood God's immanent presence, as he expressed in Psalm 139: 7-10, "Whither shall I go from thy Spirit? Or whither shall I flee from thy presence? If I ascend up into heaven, thou art there: if I make my bed in hell, behold, thou art there. If I take the wings of the morning, and dwell in the uttermost parts of the sea; Even there shall thy hand lead me, and thy right hand shall hold me." This concept of God's immensity is also found in Jeremiah 23: 23-24, "Am I a God at hand, saith the Lord, and not a God afar off? Can any hide himself in secret places that I shall not see him? Saith the Lord. Do not I fill heaven and earth? Saith the Lord."

God is eternal. He is without beginning or end, and free from all succession of time. He is the cause of time itself.[140] In Genesis 21: 33 God is referred to as; the "everlasting God". In Psalm 90: 2, Moses expresses this well, "Before the mountains were brought forth, or ever thou hadst formed the earth and the world, even from everlasting to everlasting, thou art God." God does not grow, develop, or mature. He existed before the world existed, and dwells in eternity even now. When all history has ended, He will still continue eternal.[141] The Psalmist stated in Psalm 102: 27, "But thou art the same, and thy years shall have no end." Habakkuk refers to God's eternal nature in Habakkuk 1: 12, "Art thou not from everlasting, O Lord my God, mine Holy One?..."

In saying God is infinite and eternal; we also establish that there is no limitation in His nature and essence.[142] That He is without beginning or end may be inferred from the doctrine of His self-existence; he who exists by reason of his nature rather than his volition, must always have existed, and must continue to exist forever."[143] We recognize that God is infinite in time and space, and in perfection. He is perfect in His "mode of existence", as well as in "His power, wisdom, goodness, justice, holiness, and truth."[144]

God has certain attributes that establish for us who He is. It has been said that an attribute is not a "part" of God, but it is "how God is".[145] God is omnipresent. God is present everywhere at once. "He fills it (creation), not as part to part, but the whole infinite deity is entirely, undividedly present, at each point in creation, in each moment of time. He is present in hell in the manifestation and execution of righteous wrath, while He is present in heaven, in the manifestation, and communication of gracious love and glory."[146] It has been stated that

"God is the totality of His essence, without diffusion or expansion, multiplication or division, and penetrates and fills the universe in all its parts."[147] No matter how much we may try, we cannot "escape" from God. "Neither distance nor darkness hides from Him."[148] It states in Hebrews 4: 13, "Neither is there any creature that is not manifest in his sight: but all things are naked and opened unto the eyes of Him with whom we have to do." There is nowhere anyone can go away from God. "God is a God, both at hand and afar off, so that no one can hide himself in a secret place: That perfection of God which expresses His transcendence with respect to space. This transcendent God is yet present everywhere in heaven and earth. God is Spirit; he has no body and hence is not limited by space."[149]

God is omniscient. The scope of His knowledge is infinite. He knows not only Himself perfectly, but all other things perfectly also. He knows things "immediately, simultaneously, exhaustively, and truly."[150] God's knowledge was not "acquired", and cannot be increased. Time passing, does not add to God's knowledge. Events taking place, do not bring them in front of God. Everything that is known to Him, are to Him "eternally present and known".[151] A.W. Tozer once stated about God's omniscience – "God knows instantly and effortlessly all matter and all matters, all mind and every mind, all spirit and all spirits, all being and every being, all creaturehood and all creatures, every plurality and all pluralities, all law and every law, all relations, all causes, all thoughts, all mysteries, all enigmas, all feeling, all desires, every unuttered secret, all thrones and dominions, all personalities, all things visible and invisible in heaven and in earth, motion, space, time, life, death, good, evil, heaven, and hell. Because God knows all things perfectly, He knows nothing better than any other thing, but all things equally well. He never discovers anything, He is never surprised, never amazed. He never wonders about anything nor (except when drawing men out for their own good) does He seek information or ask questions."[152]

Psalm 147: 4-5 says "He telleth the number of the stars; He calleth them all by their names. Great is our Lord, and of great power: His understanding is infinite." God knows, and is aware of everyone. Psalm 33: 13-15 says "The Lord looketh from heaven; He beholdeth all the sons of men. From the place of His habitation He looketh upon all the inhabitants of earth. He fashioneth their hearts alike; He considereth all their works." David was intimately aware of how well God knew him, as he relates in Psalm 139: 1-4 "O Lord, thou hast searched me, and known me. Thou knowest my downsitting and mine uprising, thou understandest my thought afar off. Thou compassest my path and my lying down, and art acquainted with all my ways. For there is not a word in my tongue, but, lo, O Lord, thou knowest it altogether." Someone once said of God's knowledge – "He knows the mighty principles which He first called into being to govern His creation. He knows what keeps the planets in their orbits. He knows the sparrow that falls to the ground and the violet that lifts it's dainty head in the forest. Above all, He knows you, intimately, personally, vitally. He knows your thoughts, words and deeds, and loves you still."[153]

God is omnipotent. The word omnipotent comes from the Latin word "omnis" meaning "all".[154] God has all power to execute His will. He can do everything, except whatever is contrary to His nature. Habakkuk 1: 13 teaches us that God cannot look upon iniquity. It states "Thou art of purer eyes than to behold evil, and canst not look on iniquity..." God cannot deny Himself, as it says in 2 Timothy 2: 13, "If we believe not, yet he abideth faithful: he cannot deny himself." Titus 1: 2 reminds us that God cannot lie – "In hope of eternal life, which God, that cannot lie, promised before the world began." God cannot be tempted to sin, or tempt man to sin as it says in James 1: 13, "Let no man say when he is tempted, I am tempted of God: for God cannot be tempted with evil, neither tempteth he any man."

God is immutable. He does not change. He remains the same in His "essence, attributes, consciousness, and will."[155] James 1: 17 states "Every good gift and every perfect gift is from above, and cometh down from the Father of lights, with whom is no variableness, neither shadow of turning." God stated in Malachi 3: 6, "For I am the Lord, I change not..." His counsel never changes, as it states in Psalm 33: 11, "The counsel of the Lord standeth forever, the thoughts of his heart to all generations." His promises do not change. 2 Corinthians 1: 20 reads "For all the promises of God in him are yeah, and in him Amen, unto the glory of God by us." His mercy never changes. Psalm 103: 17 states "But the mercy of the Lord is from everlasting to everlasting upon them that fear Him and His righteousness unto children's children."[156] God's immutability is "that perfection which designates God's constancy and unchangeableness in His being, decrees, and works. He remains forever the same true God, faithful to Himself, His decrees, His revelation, and His works. He undergoes no change from within, nor does He undergo change due to anything outside of Himself."[157] Considering all of God's attributes, there can be no contradiction between them. God never needs to "suspend" one attribute, in order to exercise another one. In Him, all His attributes are one. "All of God does all that God does; He does not divide Himself to perform a work, but works in the total unity of His being."[158]

We learn from the Bible that God is one, but He exists in three Persons which are called respectively; Father, Son, and Holy Spirit. These are not three individuals, but three forms in which the Divine

Being exists. Each one of the Trinity possesses the entire or whole of the divine essence. They are not "subordinate in being" one to another, but the order of existence might be said to be: the Father, the Son, and the Holy Spirit.[159]

There is no other God but God, as is found in Isaiah 45: 5, "I am the Lord, and there is none else, there is no God beside me." In Deuteronomy 6: 4 we read, "Hear, O Israel: The Lord our God is one Lord." Also in Deuteronomy 4: 35 it states, "Unto thee it was shewed, that thou mightest know that the Lord He is God; there is none else beside him." This is also taught in the New Testament. John 17: 3 says "And this is life eternal, that they might know thee the only true God, and Jesus Christ, whom thou hast sent." This is found in 1 Corinthians 8: 6, "But to us there is but one God, the Father, of whom are all things, and we in him; and one Lord Jesus Christ, by whom are all things, and we by him." 1 Timothy supports this, it reads in chapter 2 verse 5, "For there is one God, and one mediator between God and man, the man Christ Jesus."

There are hints of the existence of the Trinity, beginning even in Genesis. Genesis 1: 26 reads, "And God said, Let us make man in our image..." Genesis 3: 22 speaks similarly, "And the Lord God said, Behold, the man is become as one of us..." The Hebrew word for God is "Elohim", which is used more than any other word for God throughout the Old Testament. "Elohim" is a word which is in plural form. The plural ending is similar to the way "cherub" becomes "cherubim" or "seraph" become "seraphim". However, the singular forms for God (El and Elah), are also often used. The image of both singular and plural words for God is evidence, that God is a plurality of Persons in the Trinity.[160] B.B. Warfield defined the Trinity in the following manner, "There is one only and true God, but in the unity of the Godhead there are three coeternal and coequal Persons, the same in substance but distinct in subsistence."[161]

There are various instances in the New Testament where the Trinity is made obvious. Matthew 3: 16-17 states, "And Jesus, when He was baptized, went up straightway out of the water: and, lo, the heavens were opened unto him, and he saw the Spirit of God descending like a dove, and lighting upon Him: and lo a voice from heaven, saying, This is my beloved Son, in whom I am well pleased." All three members of the Trinity are also spoken of in Matthew 28: 19 "Go ye therefore, and teach all nations, baptizing them in the name of the Father, and of the Son, and of the Holy Ghost." They are also referred to in 1 Peter 1: 2 "Elect according to the foreknowledge of God the Father, through sanctification of the Spirit, unto obedience and sprinkling of the blood of Jesus Christ..."

Jesus even used the plural form, when speaking of Himself along with the Father and the Spirit, "We will come unto Him and make our abode with Him." It is important to think of God as Trinity in Unity, neither "confounding the Persons nor dividing the substance."[162] It states in John 14: 23, "Jesus answered and said unto him, If a man love me, he will keep my words: and my Father will love him, and we will come unto him, and make our abode with him." We see that God is revealed to us as Father, Son, and Holy Spirit, with each having distinct personal attributes, but not divided in nature, essence, or being. [163]

The Bible teaches that the work of creation was brought about by the Father (Genesis 1: 1), the Son (Col. 1: 16), and the Holy Spirit (Job 26: 13 and Psalm 104: 30). Luke 1: 35 states "...The Holy Ghost shall come upon thee, and the power of the Highest shall overshadow thee: therefore also that holy thing which shall be born of thee shall be called the Son of

God." The Trinity was a part of the Incarnation, though only the Son came to dwell among us. The Trinity is also expressed in Hebrews 9: 14, "How much more shall the blood of Christ, who through the eternal Spirit offered Himself without spot to God, purge your conscience from dead works to serve the living God."[164] It may also be said that prayer is practiced in a "Trinitarian" way. We address the Father in the name of Jesus Christ as the Holy Spirit directs us.[165] A verse that solidifies the concept and reality of the Trinity is 1 John 5: 7, "For there are three that bear record in heaven, the Father, the Word, and the Holy Ghost: and these three are one."[166]

CHAPTER 5: COVENANTS, LAW, AND GRACE

The Hebrew noun "berith" is translated to English as covenant. From the Old Testament, the word "berith" signifies three different types of legal relationships. The first is a bilateral or two-sided covenant, between two people who enter the agreement voluntarily. God never enters into this kind of covenant with men. The second type of covenant is unilateral, or one-sided, and is imposed by a superior party. God "commands" a "berith", which man is to obey. In Genesis 2: 17, we see this type of covenant in the one God made with Adam. God told him, "But of the tree of the knowledge of good and evil, thou shalt not eat of it: for in the day that thou eatest thereof, thou shalt surely die." This was a covenant of works, which Adam failed, but which "the last Adam", Jesus Christ came and fulfilled (1 Cor. 15: 45).[167]

It states in Galatians 4: 4-5, "But when the fullness of the time was come, God sent forth His Son, made of a woman, made under the law. To redeem them that were under the law, that we might receive the adoption of sons." After Adam disobeyed the covenant of works that God had made with him in the garden, God speaks of the promised seed (Jesus Christ) who would "bruise the head" of the serpent. It says in Genesis 3: 15, "And I will put enmity between thee and the woman, and between thy seed and her seed; it shall bruise thy head, and thou shalt bruise his heel." The third type of covenant is a covenant of grace. In this covenant, God imposes an obligation upon Himself. It states in Genesis 17: 7, "And I will establish my covenant between me and thee and thy seed after thee in their generations for an everlasting covenant, to be a God unto thee, and to thy seed after thee." The token of this covenant was circumcision. This covenant was ratified by God alone, and not by God and Abraham. This is described in Genesis 15: 9-17. God walked alone through the pieces of the sacrificial animals, which was traditionally done by both parties. God "swore fidelity to His promises", and "placed the obligation of their fulfillment on Himself alone." Abraham did not make an oath, as he was actually in a deep sleep at this time. So, the Abrahamic Covenant was a covenant of grace, and its fulfillment was only dependent upon what God would do.[168]

The covenant that God made with Abraham contained certain promises. The first promise is found in Genesis 12: 2, "And I will make of thee a great nation, and I will bless thee and make thy name great; and thou shalt be a blessing." In Genesis 22: 17, God promised to "multiply thy seed as the stars of the heaven, and as the sand which is upon the seashore." Genesis 12: 3 reveals God's heart for the Jewish people, as it states "I will bless them that bless thee, and curse him that curseth thee, and in thee shall all the families of the earth be blessed." God also promised to Abraham's seed, as is spoken in Genesis 15: 18, "unto thy seed have I given this land, from the river of Egypt unto the great river, the river Euphrates." And finally in Genesis 22: 18 it states "And in thy seed shall all the nations of the earth be blessed; because thou hast obeyed my voice." Abraham had obeyed God's voice in the test of faith, which God had placed before him. In Genesis 22: 2, God made a request of Abraham, "...Take now thy son, thine only son Isaac, whom thou lovest, and get thee into the land of Moriah; and offer him there for a burnt offering upon one of the mountains which I will tell thee of." Abraham responded in faithful obedience to God's request. Abraham's faith, that God would provide a sacrifice, is revealed in Genesis 22: 5, "And Abraham said unto his young men, Abide ye here with the ass; and I and the lad will go yonder and worship, and come again with you." Abraham also expressed his faith in God's provision in verse 8, "And Abraham said, My Son God will provide himself a lamb for a burnt offering..." Abraham did not need to sacrifice his son Isaac. God provided "a ram caught in a thicket", just in time. It was after this test of faith, that God pronounced the covenantal blessing of Genesis 22: 18. Truly in Abraham's seed all the nations of the earth would be blessed. In reading Galatians 3: 16, we see who the promise was to, "Now to Abraham and his seed were the promises made. He saith not, and to seeds, as of many; but as of one, and to thy seed, which is Christ." The next verse reveals an important part of the Abrahamic covenant, Galatians 3: 17 states "that the covenant, that was confirmed before of God in Christ." The security for this covenant was God's oath by Himself and His great name."[169] It states in Hebrews 6: 13, "For when God made promises to Abraham, because he could swear by no greater, he sware by himself. "God would fulfill the promises to Abraham through Himself, through sending His Son Jesus Christ. As God had the "ram caught in a thicket" waiting, to save the life of Isaac, so He had the coming of His only begotten Son as the sacrificial lamb to take away the sins of the world. Abraham called the mount that He and Isaac had visited "Jehovoh-jireh" which means "The Lord Will Provide."

God introduced a covenant of works through Moses. The Law of Moses included a moral law (Ten Commandments), a ceremonial law (sacrifices, priesthood, holy seasons, etc.) and judicial law (civil laws).[170]

This law set forth God's standards for righteousness. In all reality, though, man was unable to conform to that perfect standard. The law made man aware of how sinful and imperfect he actually was. It states in Romans 7: 7, "What shall we say then? Is the law sin? God forbid. Nay, I had not known sin, but by the law: for I had not known lust, except the law had said, Thou shalt not covet." The law condemned man in his unrighteousness, and his failure to keep the law. Romans 7: 9-11 states, "For I was alive without the law once: but when the commandment came, sin revived, and I died. And the commandment, which was ordained to life, I found to be death. For sin taking occasion by the commandment, deceived me, and by it slew me."

The Israelites, by being under the Law of Moses, were shown by the measuring stick of the law, their inability to keep the law, and ultimately of their need for a Savior. They were left without any hope within themselves; their only hope was the Savior coming to fulfill the demands of the Law. They were left without any hope within themselves and in their ability to merit salvation through their righteousness. They were made ready to long for that grace, which would remove them from the "curse" of the law. Galatians 3: 13 states, "Christ hath redeemed us from the curse of the law, being made a curse for us: for it is written, cursed is every one that hangeth on a tree." Their salvation was never intended to have come from the law. It states in Hebrews 10: 1, "For the law having a shadow of good things to come and not the very image of the things, can never with those sacrifices which they offered year by year continually make the comers thereunto perfect."

Salvation was always by faith, and not by works. Galatians 3: 24 states, "Wherefore the law was our schoolmaster to bring us unto Christ, that we might be justified by faith."[171] It states in Romans 5:1,

"Therefore being justified by faith, we have peace with God through our Lord Jesus Christ."

Through the Old Testament prophet Jeremiah, God spoke of a New Covenant which was to come. Jeremiah 31: 31-33 reads, "Behold, the days come, saith the Lord, that I will make a new covenant with the house of Israel, and with the house of Judah: Not according to the covenant that I made with their fathers in the day that I took them by the hand to bring them out of the land of Egypt; which my covenant they brake, although I was an husband unto them, saith the Lord: But this shall be the covenant that I will make with the house of Israel; After those days, saith the Lord, I will put my law in their inward parts, and write it in their hearts; and will be their God, and they shall be my people." Works were never intended to bring about salvation. Ephesians 2: 8-9 says, "For by grace are ye saved through faith; and that not of yourselves: it is the gift of God. Not of works, lest any man should boast." Jesus Christ brought an end to the covenant of works, or law, by what He did for us. Romans 10: 4 states, "For Christ is the end of the law for righteousness to everyone that believeth." He became the mediator of a "better covenant" which was based on "better promises". Hebrews 8: 6 states, "But now hath he obtained a more excellent ministry, by how much also he is the mediator of a better covenant, which was established upon better promises."

The new covenant is not based on our faithfulness to God, but on His faithfulness to us. God never found fault with His covenant or law, but the fault was found with His people. It states in Romans 7: 12 "Wherefore the law is holy and the commandment holy, and just, and good." The law was good, but those attempting to obey the law were not. They were sinners. As Paul further pointed out in Romans 7: 14 about himself, he was a sinner and of the flesh. It states, "For we know that the law is spiritual: but I am carnal, sold under sin." Paul having been a "Pharisee of the Pharisees" was well acquainted with keeping the Law of Moses, and of its inadequacies in making him righteous. The law could never change the inward nature or heart of a person. Hebrews 7: 19 states, "For the law made nothing perfect, but the bringing in of a better hope did; by the which we draw nigh unto God." The Law of Moses "declared God's holy standard", but "could not give the power needed" to obey it. Ezekiel prophesied about the aid that God would send. Ezekiel 36: 26 & 27 states, "A new heart also will I give you, and a new spirit will I put within you: and I will take away the stony heart out of your flesh, and I will give you a heart of flesh. And I will put my spirit within you, and cause you to walk in my statutes, and ye shall keep my judgments and do them."

The new covenant through the grace of Jesus Christ provides us with both a new heart, and a divine nature. This is evident in reading 2 Peter 1: 3-4, "According as his divine power hath given unto us all things that pertain unto life and godliness, through the knowledge of him that hath called us to glory and virtue: Whereby are given unto us exceeding great and precious promises: that by these ye might be partakers of the divine nature, having escaped the corruption that is in the world through lust." This new covenant is wholly and completely of grace. As we accept God's free gift of grace, to us by faith in Jesus Christ, God gives us a new nature. He indwells us with His Spirit, who also becomes our lawgiver. We can rest in His grace. Grace says "The work is done – believe and live."[172]

The covenant of grace offers a believer an "unmerited and unearned righteousness." It offers him the righteousness of Jesus Christ, which is received by faith.[173] As it states in Romans 3: 27-28, "Where is boasting then? It is excluded. By what law? Of work? Nay: but by the law of faith.

Therefore, we conclude that a man is justified by faith without the deeds of the law." Paul further points out in Romans 8: 1-4, how the believer stands uncondemned before God, as He walks "in the Spirit". It states, "There is therefore now no condemnation to them which are in Christ Jesus, who walk not after the flesh, but after the Spirit. For the law of the Spirit of life in Christ Jesus hath made me free from the law of sin and death. For what the law could not do, in that it was weak through the flesh, and for sin, condemned sin in the flesh: That the righteousness of the law might be fulfilled in us, who walk not after the flesh, but after the Spirit."

CHAPTER 6: THE CHURCH AND BIBLICAL SALVATION

The first mention of "church" in the New Testament is in Matthew. In Matthew 16: 13-18 it states, "When Jesus came into the coasts of Caesarea Philippi, He asked his disciples, saying, Whom do men say that I the Son of Man am? And they said, some say that thou art John the Baptist: some Elias; and others Jeremias, or one of the prophets. He saith unto them, But whom say ye that I am? And Simon Peter answered and said, Thou art the Christ, the Son of the living God. And Jesus answered and said unto him, Blessed art thou, Simon Barjona: for flesh and blood hath not revealed it unto thee, but my Father which is in heaven. And I say unto thee, that thou art Peter, and upon this rock I will build my church; and the gates of hell shall not prevail against it." There is debate whether the "rock" Jesus spoke of here, was Peter, Jesus Himself, or Peter's confession of Jesus' deity. The word "rock" in the Bible, is used to denote Jesus Christ, Himself. Deuteronomy 32: 3-4 states, "Because I will publish the name of the Lord: ascribe ye greatness unto our God. He is the Rock, His work is perfect: for all His ways are judgment: a God of truth and without iniquity, just and right is He." From these verses it is made evident that God is that "Rock". It says in Deuteronomy 32: 15, "...then he forsook God which made him, and lightly esteemed the Rock of His salvation." Deuteronomy 32: 17-18 says, "They sacrificed unto devils, not to God; to gods whom they knew not, to new gods that came newly up, whom your fathers feared not. Of the Rock that begat thee thou art unmindful, and hast forgotten God that formed thee. Here, the true God is spoken of as the "Rock". Deuteronomy 32: 27-31 states, "Were it not that I feared the wrath of the enemy, lest their adversaries should behave themselves strangely, and lest they should say, Our hand is high, and the Lord hath not done all this. For they are a nation void of counsel, neither is there any understanding in them. O that they were wise, that they understood this that they would consider their latter end! How should one chase a thousand, and two put ten thousand to flight, except their Rock had sold them, and the Lord had shut them up? For their rock is not as our Rock, even our enemies themselves being judges." Here, it speaks of Israel's enemies having another "rock", or another god that they followed. Israel's "Rock" was the true and living God, whereas the surrounding pagan nations served another "rock", or another god. Samuel's mother Hannah states in 1 Samuel 2: 1-2, "My heart rejoiceth in the Lord, mine horn is exalted in the Lord: My mouth is enlarged over mine enemies; because I rejoice in thy salvation. There is none holy as the Lord: for there is none beside thee: neither is there any rock like our God." It is clear here, that she is referring to the Lord, as a "Rock". David spoke of the Lord as "my rock" after he was delivered out of Saul's hands. It states in 2 Samuel 22: 1-2, "And David spake unto the Lord the words of this song, in the day that the Lord had delivered him out of the hand of all his enemies, and out of the hand of Saul: And he said, The Lord is my rock, and my fortress, and my deliverer." Later in this same chapter, David speaks of God as a "rock". It states in 2 Samuel 22: 32, "For who is God, save the Lord? And who is a rock, save our God? He reiterates this point again in verse 47, "The Lord liveth: and blessed be my rock; and exalted be the God of the rock of my salvation."

The Book of Psalms is filled with verses that refer to God as a "rock". It states in Psalm 18: 2, "The Lord is my rock, and my fortress, and my deliverer; my God, my strength, in whom I will trust; my buckler, and the horn of my salvation, and my high tower." Psalm 42: 9 states, "I will say unto God my rock, why go I mourning because of the oppression of the enemy?" It states in Psalm 61: 1-3, "Hear my cry, O God; attend unto my prayer. From the end of the earth will I cry unto thee, when my heart is overwhelmed: lead me to the rock that is higher than I, for thou hast been a shelter for me, and a strong tower from the enemy." David refers to God as a "rock", again in Psalm 62: 6-7, "He only is my rock and my salvation; He is my defense; I shall not be moved. In God is my salvation and my glory: the rock of my strength, and my refuge, is in God." Speaking of the children of Israel in the wilderness, and some of their experiences there, Psalm 78: 35 states, "And they remembered that God was their rock, and the high God their redeemer." The same concept is established in Psalm 92: 15, "To shew that the Lord is upright: He is my rock, and there is no unrighteousness in Him"

Isaiah speaks of the Lord as a "rock of offence" in Isaiah 8: 13-14, "Sanctify the Lord of Hosts Himself; and let Him be your fear, and let Him be your dread. And He shall be for a sanctuary; but for a stone of stumbling and for a rock of offence to both the houses of Israel, for a gin and for a snare to the inhabitants of Jerusalem." Paul, in Romans 9: 33 makes a similar reference to the one Isaiah did as he states, "As it is written, Behold, I lay in Sion a stumbling stone and rock of offence: and whosoever believeth on him shall not be ashamed." The "him" Paul spoke of here is Jesus Christ. Paul in 1 Corinthians 10: 4, speaking of their "fathers" who were "under the cloud" and "passed through the sea," said of them, "And did all drink the same spiritual drink: for they drank of that spiritual Rock that followed them: and that Rock was Christ." Paul clearly identified that "rock" as being Jesus Christ.

Peter, after being indwelt with God's Spirit at Pentecost, and becoming emboldened by God's Spirit, stated in 1 Peter 2: 4-8, "To whom coming, as unto a living stone, disallowed indeed of men, but chosen of God, and precious, Ye also, as lively stones, are built up a spiritual house, an holy priesthood, to offer up spiritual sacrifices, acceptable to God by Jesus Christ. Wherefore, also is contained in the Scripture, Behold, I lay in Sion a chief cornerstone, elect, precious: and he that believeth on Him shall not be confounded. Unto you therefore which believe He is precious: but unto them which be disobedient the stone which the builders disallowed, the same is made the head of the corner, And a stone of stumbling and a rock of offense, even to them which stumble at the word, being disobedient: whereunto also they were appointed." If Peter, himself, had been the rock that Jesus was referring to in Matthew chapter 16, it is strange that Peter would refer to Jesus here, as a stone of stumbling and a rock of offense.

Peter's confession in Matthew 16: 16, "...Thou art the Christ, the Son of the living God" was given to Peter, not by man, but by the Father. Jesus said in Matthew 16: 17, "...Blessed art thou, Simon Barjona: for flesh and blood hath not revealed it unto thee, but my Father which is in heaven." The Father revealed who Jesus was to Peter. Peter's true confession and understanding of Jesus being the Christ, the Son of the living God, did not come to Peter from man, but from God. In this same way, in the days to come, the Spirit of God would bear witness to people, about who Jesus is, and through the witness of the Spirit, they too, like Peter, would confess that Jesus is the Christ, the Son of the living God. Peter, after Pentecost, and after healing the lame man by the gate of the temple, spoke to Annas the high priest, Caiphas, John & Alexander and the kindred of the high priest and said "Be it known unto you all, and to all the people of Israel, that by the name of Jesus Christ of Nazareth, whom ye crucified, whom God raised from the dead, even by Him doth this man stand here before you whole. This is the stone which was set at nought of you builders, which is become the head of the corner. Neither is there salvation in any other: for there is none other name under heaven given among men, whereby we must be saved" (Acts 4: 10-12). Once again, we see that Peter refers to Jesus as the stone. Peter was not the stone, Jesus was. Jesus would build his church – His body of called out believers, on the confession of His deity, similar to that confession that Peter had professed at Caesarea Philippi. It says in 1 Cor. 12: 3, "Where fore I give you to understand that no man speaking by the Spirit of God calleth Jesus accursed: and that no man can say that Jesus is the Lord, but by the Holy Ghost." As Jesus had told Peter, flesh and blood had not revealed to Peter that Jesus was the Christ, but His Father in heaven had revealed it to Peter. Now, during this age of grace we live in, God's Spirit reveals this truth to people, and in this way Jesus is forming His church upon the earth. Jesus taught in John chapter 3 that a man must be born of the Spirit to enter into the kingdom of God. He stated in John 3: 5-8, "...Verily, verily I say unto thee, except a man be born of water and of the Spirit, he cannot enter into the kingdom of God. That which is born of the flesh is flesh; and that which is born of the Spirit is spirit. Marvel not that I said unto thee, Ye must be born again. The wind bloweth where it listeth, and thou hearest the sound thereof, but canst not tell whence it cometh, and whither it goeth: so is everyone that is born of the Spirit." Jesus told His disciples, that He would send the Spirit,

"And I will pray the Father and he shall give you another Comforter, that he may abide with you forever; even the Spirit of truth; whom the world cannot receive, because it seeth him not, neither knoweth him; for he dwelleth with you and shall be in you" (John 14: 16-17). It says in Ephesians 2: 22, "In whom ye also are builded together for an habitation of God through the Spirit." After the day of Pentecost, God began forming His church, through His Spirit bearing witness to people of Jesus Christ and His deity, and by His Spirit indwelling the hearts of believers. His Spirit began to reign, not in a temple made with hands, but in the hearts of men. It says in Ephesians 3: 17, "That Christ may dwell in your hearts by faith; that ye, being rooted and grounded in love." It says in Ephesians 5: 29-30, "For no man ever yet hated his own flesh; but nourisheth it and cherisheth it, even as the Lord the church: For we are members of His body, of His flesh, and of His bones." It teaches in Genesis 2: 23, "And Adam said, This is now bone of my bones, and flesh of my flesh." in speaking of Eve, "she shall be called Woman, because she was taken out of Man." In the same way, we – the church – the "body" of Christ, was taken out of Christ. He sent His Spirit to indwell men's hearts after He ascended to heaven. Even though we are in the world, we are part of His body by being indwelt by His Holy Spirit. It states in 1 Cor. 6: 19-20, "What? Know ye not that your body is the temple of the Holy Ghost which is in you, which ye have of God, and ye are not your own? For ye are bought with a price: therefore glorify God in your body, and in your spirit, which are God's."

The Church of Jesus Christ in the world today is a spiritual entity. Although we attend "church" in different kinds of buildings, the church is the "body" of Jesus Christ made up of born again believers from different denominations. It is not a political organization or kingdom. Jesus said in John 18: 36, "My kingdom is not of this world: if my kingdom were of this world, then would my servants fight, that I should not be delivered to the Jews: but now is my kingdom not from hence."

Jesus, speaking to the Pharisees about when the kingdom of God should come, said "The Kingdom of God cometh not with observation: Neither shall they say, Lo here! Or, lo there! For, behold, the kingdom of God is within you" (Luke 17: 20-21). The only place the kingdom of God is located on earth today, is in men's hearts. Paul wrote to the Colossians saying "Giving thanks unto the Father, which hath made us meet to be partakers of the inheritance of the saints in light: who hath delivered us from the power of darkness, and hath translated us into the kingdom of his dear Son: In whom we have redemption through his blood, even the forgiveness of sins: who is the image of the invisible God, the firstborn of every creature: For by him were all things created, that are in heaven, and that are in earth, visible and invisible, whether they be thrones, or dominions, or principalities, or powers: all things were created by him, and for him: And he is before all things, and by him all things consist. And he is the head of the body, the church: who is the beginning, the firstborn from the dead: that in all things he might have the preeminence" (Col. 1: 12-18). The kingdom of God, as it says in Romans 14: 17, "is not meat and drink; but righteousness, and peace, and joy in the Holy Ghost." There is absolutely no indication in the New Testament that the Kingdom of God is a political kingdom existing on earth today. The Kingdom of God on the earth today is a spiritual kingdom.

Daniel speaks of a coming kingdom, which will never be destroyed, and not be left to other people, but consume and break into pieces all other kingdoms of this world. Daniel 2: 44-45 states, "And in the days of these kings shall the God of heaven set up a kingdom, which shall never be destroyed: and the kingdom shall not be left to other people, but it shall break in pieces and consume all these kingdoms, and it shall stand forever. Forasmuch as thou sawest that the stone was cut out of the mountain without hands, and that it brake in pieces the iron, the brass, the clay, the silver, and the gold." When Jesus returns to sit on His throne in Jerusalem, and to reign during the millennium for one thousand years as King of Kings, he shall tear down all other kingdoms of the prince of this world. It states in Revelation 11: 15, "And the seventh angel sounded; and there were great voices in heaven saying, The Kingdoms of this world are become the kingdoms of our Lord, and of His Christ; and He shall reign forever and ever."

The biblical "plan of salvation" is as follows: The Bible says we are all sinners. Romans 3: 23 says all have sinned and fall short of the glory of God. We simply just do not, and cannot measure up to God's standard, to enter heaven and dwell in His presence. God, of course, knowing man would fall before he was ever created, made a way to redeem man back to Himself, by coming to earth in the form of a man. God speaks of this in Genesis 3: 15. He says to the serpent (Satan), that He will put enmity between you and the woman, between your seed and her seed. "He shall bruise your head and you shall bruise his heel." Isaiah says Jesus is God, incarnate (God in flesh). In chapter 9 verse 6, Isaiah says "Unto us a child (Jesus) is born, unto us a Son (Jesus) is given; and the government will be upon His shoulder and His name will be called Wonderful, Counselor, Mighty God (God), Everlasting Father (God), Prince of Peace. Christianity is the only religion that recognizes that God came down to man, in the form of a man. All other religions have man struggle to reach up and please God. Jesus pleased God for us in giving Himself as a sacrifice.

Sin is committed in the flesh, and since sin is of the flesh, sin must be overcome in the flesh. No man could be a pleasing sacrifice to God, because all men are born of the seed of fallen man. So the seed of the perfect sacrifice had to come from God, which is what Genesis 3: 15 is saying, when it says; the seed is from the woman who was to bring forth the Son of God, by the Holy Spirit (not by a sinful fallen man). In Matthew 1: 18, God says Mary's child, and her pregnancy, were brought about by the Holy Spirit. This was what Isaiah was speaking of in Isaiah 7: 14. God's Word says, "therefore the Lord Himself will give you a sign: Behold the virgin shall conceive and bear a Son, and shall call His name Immanuel." Immanuel means "God with us" (Jesus is God). All other religions strip Jesus of His glory and His deity by saying He is not God. Salvation was made possible only by a Holy God becoming flesh, offering His own life and blood as a perfect sacrifice on the cross at Calvary, in order to redeem man from his fallen state. To bring man back into that relationship with Him, that Adam and Eve enjoyed in the garden before the fall, He came and gave Himself as our Savior, so that we could put on His righteousness, made possible by what He did on the cross. He desires for us to have a personal relationship with Him, and to dwell with Him in heaven after we die.

If Satan can convince people that Jesus is not God, but just another one of many of God's sons, then he has taken away their only hope of salvation. Jesus profoundly proclaimed to be God in the Bible. If a person does not believe that Jesus is who He says He is – God, they will die in their sins without forgiveness. Satan has convinced many people, that Jesus is not who He says He is. John 1: 1 says, "In the beginning was the Word (Jesus), and the Word (Jesus) was with God, and the Word was God. John 1: 14 says, "and the Word became flesh and dwelt among us and we beheld His glory, the glory as of the only begotten of the Father, full of grace and truth."

Salvation comes through Christ and Christ alone. John 1:12 says, "but as many as received Him, to them He gave the right to become children of God, to those who believe on His name. His name is Immanuel (God with us).

God does not make salvation complicated. All we need to do is believe He is who He says He is, realize we are a sinner, and in need of a Savior, ask Him to save us, and He will. In referring back to Romans 3: 23, it says all have sinned. Romans 3: 10-12 says, "...there is none righteous, no, not one: there is none that understandeth, there is none that seeketh after God. They are all gone out of the way, they are together become unprofitable; there is none that doeth good, no, not one." Romans 3: 36 says, "He who believes in the Son has everlasting life; and he who does not believe the Son shall not see life, but the wrath of God abides on him."

Paul says in Romans 10: 6, "But the righteousness of faith speaks in this way, righteousness comes from faith in what Christ did and not from works. Paul says in Romans 10: 8, "But what does it say that is the word of faith which we preach" (Gospel by faith in Christ). Paul goes on to explain in Romans 10: 9-10, how we obtain salvation. He says if you confess with your mouth the Lord Jesus, and believe in your heart that God has raised Him from the dead, you will be saved. For with the heart one believes unto righteousness, and with the mouth confession is made unto salvation. Verse 13 says, "For whosoever calls on the name of the Lord shall be saved."

We may attend a church and hear the simple message of salvation. However, salvation does not come through any church organization, regardless of its denomination. Salvation and eternal life come only through accepting Jesus Christ as your personal Savior, accepting His payment on the cross, His shed blood, given as a free gift of grace, in His doing what we could not do for ourselves. There is nothing we can do to merit our own salvation. He has done it all.

The New Testament is the New Covenant that Jesus Christ (God), has made with believers. This covenant is based on belief in the atoning sacrifice of God (Jesus Christ) for our sins, belief that only in Him is there salvation, and asking Him to save us. Under the Old Covenant or Old Testament, there was a need for a high Priest to represent the children of Israel and offer a sacrifice for their sins. Under the New Covenant or New Testament, Jesus Christ is our high Priest. Hebrews 4: 14 says, "Seeing then that we have a great high Priest, that is passed into the heavens, Jesus the Son of God, let us hold fast our profession." Under the New Covenant or New Testament, there is no longer a need for a high Priest, to offer any sacrifice in a temple. Jesus Christ, who is God, gave Himself as that last and great sacrifice, to fulfill the law which had been given to Moses on Mount Sinai. We now live in an age of grace, not law, where by faith in what God did for us in paying for our sins, and recognizing we are sinners (having all been affected by the fall of Adam), turning to God and asking Him to save us, He will indwell us with His Holy Spirit. Then His Spirit will be our lawgiver. Hebrews 10: 16 says, "This is the covenant that I will make with them after those days, saith the Lord, I will put my laws into their hearts, and in their minds will I write them. We do not need anyone to represent us before God. Hebrews 4: 16 says, "Let us therefore come boldly unto the throne of grace that we may obtain mercy, and find grace to help in time of need. We then will have a personal relationship with God.

As believers in Jesus Christ, we will do good works. These good works follow salvation, after God's Spirit quickens a man's heart, and actually literally transforms him into a new creature. 2 Corinthians 5: 17 says, "Therefore if any man be in Christ, he is a new creature: old things are passed away; behold all things are become new." We cannot transform ourselves, a church cannot transform us, and man's wisdom cannot transform us. Only God coming into our hearts through His Holy Spirit, can transform us. He can give us a new nature. His Holy Spirit will then make us into the image of Christ. It is not something we do, it is something He does. We will then experience the true fruits of the Spirit. These fruits are spoken of in Galatians 5: 22-23, "But the fruit of the Spirit is love, joy, peace, longsuffering, gentleness, goodness, faith, meekness, temperance: against such there is no law."

Paul speaks throughout the New Testament about false teachers bringing "another gospel". What was that "other gospel"? Paul says in Galatians 1: 6, "I marvel that ye are so soon removed from Him that called you into the grace of Christ unto another gospel." That "other gospel" that was being preached, was one of works. There were false teachers saying that people needed to do certain works to obtain salvation. This was a perversion of the freedom, which God intended for us to have, by faith in Jesus Christ alone. Freedom in Christ is not freedom to sin, but freedom to allow God's Spirit to direct our lives, and for God to transform us, and not the false ideas of men to do so. God created us, God wants to save us, and God wants to guide us personally. If we believe lies about salvation, and what is needed for salvation, we are turned away from God. True freedom in Jesus Christ, can only come from coming to accept His free gift of salvation for us, and truly coming to know who He is. What Paul said to the Galatians in Galatians 2: 16, is every bit as true today as it was then..., "Knowing that a man is not justified by the works of the law, but by the faith of Jesus Christ, even we have believed in Jesus Christ, that we might be justified by the faith of Christ, and not by the works of the law: for by the works of the law shall no flesh be justified." Justified means to be brought back into a right relationship with God, after what occurred in the fall. Only faith in Christ will do this. Sanctification is the purification process that follows justification. This process comes about, not by what we do, but by what God's Spirit does in us. We cannot sanctify ourselves. We have no power to do so. We must yield to God's Spirit within us, and allow God to transform us into the image of Jesus Christ.

ENDNOTES

[1] John Ankerberg, Dillon Burroughs, How Do We Know the Bible is True (Chattanooga: AMG Publishers, 2008) 21.

[2] Ankerberg 21.

[3] Ankerberg 21.

[4] Ankerberg 21.

[5] Ankerberg 21.

[6] Ankerberg 21.

[7] Norman L. Geisler, William E. Nix, From God to Us How We God our Bible (Chicago: Moody Press, 1974) 12.

[8] Geisler, From God to Us 13.

[9] Geisler, From God to Us 13-14.

[10] John McArthur, Jr, Why I Trust the Bible (Wheaton: Victor Books, 1987) 29.

[11] McArthur 29-30.

[12] McArthur 30.

[13] McArthur 33.

[14] Norman L. Geisler, William E. Nix, A General Introduction to the Bible (Chicago: Moody Press, 1968) 235-236.

[15] Geisler, A General Introduction 235-236.

[16] Ankerberg 14.

[17] Ankerberg 45.

[18] Ankerberg 45.

[19] Josh McDowell, Evidence for Christianity Historical Evidences for the Christian Faith (Nashville: Thomas Nelson Publishers, 2006) 61-63.

[20] McDowell, Evidence for Christianity 61-63.

[21] McDowell, Evidence for Christianity 59-60.

[22] McDowell, Evidence for Christianity 59-60.

[23] McDowell, Evidence for Christianity 59-60.

[24] McDowell, Evidence for Christianity 80-91.

[25] McDowell, Evidence for Christianity 80-91.

[26] Erwin W. Lutzer, Seven Reasons Why You Can Trust the Bible (Chicago: Moody Press, 1998) 78.

[27] McDowell, Evidence for Christianity 75-80.

[28] McDowell, Evidence for Christianity 91-93.

[29] McDowell, Evidence for Christianity 91-93.

[30] McDowell, Evidence for Christianity 91-93.

[31] Lutzer, 68.
[32] Lutzer, 69.
[33] Lutzer, 74.
[34] Irving L. Jensen, Journey of the Bible (Minneapolis: World Wide Publications, 1990) 90-91.
[35] Jensen, 88.
[36] Jensen, 69.
[37] Geisler, A General Introduction 134.
[38] Lutzer, 43.
[39] Lutzer, 44-46.
[40] Lutzer, 46-48.
[41] Lutzer, 48-49.
[42] Lutzer, 48-49.
[43] Lutzer, 50.
[44] Lutzer, 51.
[45] McDowell, Evidence for Christianity 42-47.
[46] Geisler, A General Introduction 134.
[47] Geisler, A General Introduction 133.
[48] Geisler, A General Introduction 136-137.
[49] Geisler, A General Introduction 136-137.
[50] McDowell, Evidence for Christianity 42-47.
[51] Geisler, A General Introduction 137-138.
[52] Geisler, A General Introduction 148.
[53] Geisler, A General Introduction 149.
[54] Geisler, A General Introduction 154-155.
[55] Geisler, A General Introduction 161.
[56] Geisler, A General Introduction 219.
[57] Geisler, A General Introduction 220.
[58] Geisler, A General Introduction 220.
[59] Geisler, A General Introduction 138-145.
[60] Geisler, A General Introduction 220-221.
[61] Geisler, A General Introduction 146.
[62] Geisler, A General Introduction 181-183.
[63] McDowell, Evidence for Christianity 42-47.
[64] Jensen, 58.
[65] Jensen, 76.
[66] Jensen, 81-82.

[67] Jensen, 62-63.

[68] Jensen, 85-87.

[69] Jensen, 89-90.

[70] Jensen, 91-94.

[71] Norman L. Geisler, Inerrancy (Grand Rapids: Zondervan, 1980) 357-359.

[72] Geisler, Inerrancy 361.

[73] MacArthur, 25.

[74] Jensen, 40-41.

[75] MacArthur, 34-35.

[76] MacArthur, 35-36.

[77] MacArthur, 36-38.

[78] Lutzer, 57.

[79] Lutzer, 201.

[80] MacArthur, 103.

[81] MacArthur, 103-104.

[82] Henry Clarence Thiessen, Lectures in Systematic Theology (Grand Rapids: William B. Eerdmans, 1979) 13.

[83] H.I. Hester, The Heart of Hebrew History – A Study of the Old Testament (Liberty: The Quality Press, 1962) 273.

[84] Hester, 273.

[85] Hester, 273-274.

[86] Hester, 274.

[87] Hester, 275.

[88] Hester, 278.

[89] Charles C. Ryrie, Basic Theology (Wheaton: Victor Books, 1986) 254.

[90] Ryrie, 257.

[91] Louis Berkhof, Summary of Christian Doctrine (Grand Rapids: Wm. B. Eerdmans, 1938) 106-107.

[92] Augustus Hopkins Strong, Systematic Theology (Westwood: Fleming H. Revell, 1907) 711.

[93] Lewis Sperry Chafer, Systematic Theology – Soteriology, Vol. 3 (Dallas: Dallas Seminary Press, 1948) 19-21.

[94] Carl F.H. Henry, Basic Christian Doctrines (New York: Holt, Rinehart and Winston, 1962) 148-149.

[95] Strong, 711-712.

[96] Chafer, 17-18.

[97] Chafer, 19-21.

[98] Chafer, 19-21.

[99] Charles F. Pfeiffer, John Rea, Howard F. Vos, <u>Wycliffe Bible Dictionary</u> (Peabody: Henrickson Publishers, 1998) 1394-1395.

[100] Henry, 159.

[101] Henry, 160.

[102] Pfeiffer, 1396.

[103] Chafer, 26.

[104] Chafer, 26-27.

[105] Henry, 149.

[106] Henry, 150.

[107] Ryrie, 257-258.

[108] Chafer, 29.

[109] Henry, 160-161.

[110] Henry, 149.

[111] Thiessen, 248.

[112] Berkhof, <u>Summary of Christian Doctrine</u> 107-108.

[113] Louis Berkhof, <u>Systematic Theology</u> (Grand Rapids: Wm. B. Erdmans, 1941) 400.

[114] Henry, 162.

[115] Henry, 163-164.

[116] Chafer, 251.

[117] Chafer, 28.

[118] Pfeiffer, 1518.

[119] Pfeiffer, 1672-1675.

[120] Merrill C. Tenney, <u>The Zondervan Pictorial Bible Dictionary</u> (Grand Rapids: Zondervan Publishing House, 1963) 782.

[121] Pfeiffer, 1654.

[122] Pfeiffer, 1654.

[123] Pfeiffer, 1654.

[124] Warren W. Wiersbe, <u>The Wiersbe Bible Commentary – Old Testament</u> (Colorado Springs: David C. Cook, 2007) 627.

[125] Wiersbe, <u>Commentary – Old Testament</u> 203.

[126] Wiersbe, <u>Commentary – Old Testament</u> 628.

[127] Warren W. Wiersbe <u>The Wiersbe Bible Commentary – New Testament</u> (Colorado Springs: David C. Cook, 2007) 235.

[128] Pfeiffer, 1767-1768.

[129] Tenney, 830.

[130] Pfeiffer, 1672.

[131] Robin Lane Fox, Pagans and Christians (New York: Alfred A. Knopf, 1989) 33.

[132] Berkhof, Summary of Christian Doctrine 28.

[133] Theissen, 75-77.

[134] Theissen, 77.

[135] Theissen, 78.

[136] A.W. Tozer, The Knowledge of the Holy (New York: Harper & Brothers, 1961) 23.

[137] Henry, Basic Christian Doctrines 23-24.

[138] Theissen, 78.

[139] Theissen, 78.

[140] Theissen. 78.

[141] Henry, Basic Christian Doctrines 24.

[142] James Petigrew Boyce, Abstract of Systematic Theology (Philadelphia: American Baptist Publication Society, 1887) 68.

[143] Theissen, 78.

[144] Boyce, 68.

[145] Tozer, 23.

[146] Boyce, 72.

[147] Strong, Systematic Theology 279.

[148] Theissen, 80.

[149] Henry, Basic Christian Doctrines 25.

[150] Theissen, 81.

[151] Boyce, 87.

[152] Ryrie, Basic Theology 41-42.

[153] Harold Lindsell and Charles J. Woodbridge, A Handbook of Christian Truth (Old Tappan: Fleming H. Revell, 1953) 54.

[154] Lindsell, 53.

[155] Theissen, 83.

[156] Theissen, 83.

[157] Henry, Basic Christian Doctrines 25.

[158] Tozer, 23.

[159] Berkhof, Summary of Christian Doctrine 42.

[160] William M. Smith, Bible Doctrines (Indianapolis: Pilgrim Publishing House, 1951) 10.

[161] Ryrie, Basic Theology 53.

[162] Tozer, 28.

[163] Boyce, 125.

[164] Tozer, 31.

[165] Ryrie, Basic Theology 59.

[166] Smith, Bible Doctrines 12.

[167] Tenney, 186.

[168] Ryrie, Basic Theology 454-455.

[169] Pfeiffer, 388.

[170] Hester, 125.

[171] Tenney, 477.

[172] Wiersbe, The Wiersbe Bible Commentary – The New Testament 826.

[173] Henry, Basic Christian Doctrines 97-98.

ABOUT THE AUTHOR

Shawna K. Lindsey was a Mormon from 1979 until 2009. While not attending the Mormon Church in 1983, she was witnessed to by a relative and became a born again believer in Jesus Christ Not knowing enough about the Bible, she went back to the Mormon Church in 1984 as a brand new Christian. She was married in the Salt Lake City Temple in 1984, and did Mormon temple work in many temples over the next 23 years. God miraculously opened her eyes to the truth of Mormonism on Easter Sunday 2009, after a year of intensive instruction and study of the New Testament. She now speaks publicly about the hidden doctrines of Mormonism, its little known seditious history, and its similarity to Islam. She has a law degree and a doctorate in Theology.

www.ingramcontent.com/pod-product-compliance
Lightning Source LLC
Chambersburg PA
CBHW070535030426
42337CB00016B/2213